SCORING CHART

Points	Three doubles			Four doubles			Five doubles		
	× 1	× 4	× 6	× 1	× 4	× 6	× 1	× 4	× 6
20	160	640	960	320	1280	1920	640	2560	3840
22	180	710	1050	350	1400	2100	700	2810	4230
24	190	760	1140	380	1530	2310	770	3080	4620
26	210	840	1260	420	1670	2490	830	3320	4980
28	220	890	1350	450	1800	2700	900	3590	5370
30	240	960	1440	480	1920	2880	960	3840	5760
32	260	1030	1530	510	2040	3060	1020	4090	6150
34	270	1080	1620	540	2170	3270	1090	4360	6540
36	290	1160	1740	580	2310	3450	1150	4600	6900
38	300	1210	1830	610	2440	3660	1220	4870	7290
40	320	1280	1920	640	2560	3840	1280	5120	7680
42	340	1350	2010	670	2680	4020	1340	5370	8070
44	350	1400	2100	700	2810	4230	1410	5640	8460
46	370	1480	2200	740	2950	4410	1470	5880	8820
48	380	1530	2310	770	3080	4620	1540	6150	9210
50	400	1600	2400	800	3200	4800	1600	6400	9600
52	420	1670	2490	830	3320	4980	1660	6650	9990
54	430	1720	2580	860	3450	5190	1730	6920	10380
56	450	1800	2700	900	3590	5370	1790	7160	10740
58	460	1850	2790	930	3720	5580	1860	7430	11130
60	480	1920	2880	960	3840	5760	1920	7680	11520
62	500	1990	2970	990	3960	5940	1980	7930	11910
64	510	2040	3060	1020	4090	6150	2050	8200	12300
66	530	2120	3180	1060	4230	6330	2110	8440	12660
68	540	2170	3270	1090	4360	6540	2180	8710	13050
70	560	2240	3360	1120	4480	6720	2240	8960	13440
72	580	2310	3450	1150	4600	6900	2300	9210	13830
74	590	2360	3540	1180	4730	7100	2370	9480	14220
76	610	2440	3660	1220	4870	7290	2430	9720	14580
78	620	2480	3750	1250	5000	7500	2500	9990	14970
80	640	2560	3840	1280	5120	7680	2560	10240	15360

A Mah Jong Handbook

ELEANOR NOSS WHITNEY

A 一萬 二萬 三萬 四萬 伍萬 六萬 七萬 八萬 九萬

MAH JONG
HANDBOOK

How to Play, Score, and Win the Modern Game

CHARLES E. TUTTLE COMPANY
Rutland, Vermont & Tokyo, Japan

Published by the Charles E. Tuttle Company, Inc.
of Rutland, Vermont & Tokyo, Japan
with editorial offices at
Suido 1-chome, 2-6, Bunkyo-ku, Tokyo, Japan

Copyright in Japan, 1964
by Charles E. Tuttle Co., Inc.
All Rights Reserved
First edition 1964
Twenty-eighth printing, 1997

Library of Congress Catalog Card No. 64-17162
International Standard Book No. 0-8048-0392-7

PRINTED IN SINGAPORE

Table of Contents

Part Two: Alternatives, Variations, and Additions

Part Three: Strategy

Introduction

Mah Jong has a long and puzzling history, largely obscured by uneducated guesses as to its origin, and clouded by legends. It has for centuries been the favorite game of the Chinese, and tradition has it that its name is apropos of the sound made by the tiles clicking together during the game. *Mah* means flax or hemp plant, and is said to refer to the sound of the plant's leaves clicking in the wind. *Jong* means sparrow, and supposedly recalls the chattering of the bird.

Whatever its early history is, the game found its way from China to America in the early nineteen twenties, and there experienced a fad which lasted well into the thirties. Almost simultaneously it was introduced into Japan, and became immensely popular. Like so many other Chinese things it has found its home and flowering here, and today the Japanese are the foremost players of the game.

In the long course of its development, Mah Jong has shown itself to be remarkably adaptable to all kinds of tastes, and has evolved an extraordinary number of variations. Although basically a simple game, it has become widely known in its more complicated forms, among which the American "cleared hand" and "one-double" games and the Japanese "riichi" variety are the most famous.

The experience of watching one of these varieties of Mah Jong for the first time is bewildering. The terms are incomprehensible and seem innumerable, the play among experts is usually so fast-moving that it seems impossible to follow its progress. No wonder the newcomer to Mah Jong refuses to believe the old hand's assurance that it is really a very easy game.

Significantly, however, none of these offshoots have retained their popularity for long. The case of American Mah Jong is typical. The fad of the thirties soon died out, not due to a flaw in the game itself, but because it was not originally adopted in its pure form. As first introduced to America, it was shorn of many of the features which made it such a stimulating and enduringly popular game in China. As a result, it soon became burdened with a mass of additions contributed by various American players who found it unsatisfactory in its "original" form. A number of authorities appeared, who differed from one another so widely that disputes about the rules became a great hindrance to its popularity. The terminology varied widely and increasingly from book to book (the game itself was known variously as Ma Jongg, Ma Cheuk, etc.), and it was not until late in the period that a standardized version both of rules and of terms was agreed upon by the authorities. By that time the groups of players in various parts of the country had lost their enthusiasm for learning, or unlearning, rules, and soon returned to bridge.

The story of Mah Jong in Japan is similar, but fortunately a group of interested and expert players have codified the rules of the pure game, and made them available to the public, so that true Mah Jong has been able to remain undamaged by changes introduced in other quarters. The members of the Japan Mah Jong Association are in accord in abiding by these rules, and it is among them that the game has proven most lasting.

The Association rules are revised every five or six years, to keep the game up-to-date and to incorporate those rules for which there is the greatest demand among expert players. In its latest revision, the Association has distilled a new Mah Jong game from the confusion of popular use which it calls "riichi" Mah Jong, and which it has recognized and standardized reluctantly. The original, "true" Mah Jong, has thus been kept free of superfluous details.

There has long been a need for a book to do for America what tradition has done in China, and the Mah Jong Association has done for Japan. It is my hope that this handbook will fill this need. An original creation is not in order, and I have not made one. It is the true Mah Jong game, as codified by the Japan Mah Jong Association, that is described here, although as explained below, all the variations with which I am familiar are also presented.

Players who know any of the various forms of Mah Jong may be interested to know in what particulars they contrast with the game here presented. The differences that American players will notice are mostly due to the fact that the game of the thirties was "adapted" from the Chinese and was not entirely true to the original, and partly due to the gradual simplification the game has undergone at the hands of the Japan Mah Jong Association.

Differences from the Mixed-Hand Game: In the American mixed-hand game, points were exchanged between all four players at the end of each hand; in the true game, the score is given only to the winner. Thus the goal is to go out; no benefits accrue to the player who collects high-scoring sets and takes too long doing it. This makes the two games differ considerably in character. The latter moves faster, and all one's ingenuity is required to play defensively and keep one's opponents from going out, as well as to make a "ready" hand and go out as soon as possible oneself. This greatly increases the amount of skill necessary to be a consistent winner, and decreases the role of luck in the game.

In the mixed-hand game it was the custom for all three losers always to pay the winner when he went out. The Japan Mah Jong Association has adopted the rule that if a player goes out on a discarded tile, he must be paid only by the person who discarded the tile, and not by the other players. Thus any player who is careless brings disaster down upon himself alone; the others do not suffer for his irresponsibility. This heightens the intensity of the end-game, and makes it more suspenseful and exciting, as well as making good defensive technique indispensable to successful play.

Another difference is that "chow" may be declared only for a tile discarded on the player's left, not for any tile, as was previously the case in America. Actually, this rule has always been in effect in the Oriental games, but was omitted in the first introduction of Mah Jong to America. It is one of the principal bases of defensive play, for it makes it necessary for each player to take the primary responsibility for preventing the player on his right from completing his hand too readily.

Another is that the procedures for setting up the game and beginning to play have been simplified. The discs are no longer found in most Mah Jong sets. The custom of maintaining a pair of "loose tiles" at the dead end of the wall has been abandoned. The new scoring system is greatly simplified. These and other factors have made it possible to spend a maximum of time playing, and a minimum negotiating.

Also, the flower and season tiles are no longer used. Their effect was comparable to that which would obtain if "jokers" were introduced into bridge. Leaving them out eliminates the dependence upon a few lucky draws which so plagued the game as it was played in some circles in the thirties.

Differences from the One-Double Game: The one-double game, an American variant of the mixed-hand game, provided a minimum score, without which a player might not go out. This rule limited the strategical element of Mah Jong, making it impossible for players to construct low-scoring hands when conditions dictated this procedure as advisable. The rule is not in force in the Japan Mah Jong Association code.

Differences from the Cleared-Hand Game: The rules of the cleared-hand game, a still stricter American variant, specified that a player might not go out without having achieved one of a small number of very high-scoring hands. This restricted the players' ingenuity still further and made the game almost entirely a matter of chance; it is not recognized by the Japan Mah Jong Association.

Differences from the Riichi Game: "Riichi" Mah Jong is the Japanese variety of the game in which the "ready" declaration is used. This single factor so changes the character of the game that the entire scoring system has had to be revised to accommodate it. The task was undertaken by the Mah Jong Association with some success in 1956, but it will be a long time before "riichi" Mah Jong is equipped with a truly equitable set of playing and scoring rules. When it has matured, the American public may adopt it enthusiastically, but in my opinion it would be hasty to import it now.

PURPOSE AND PLAN

It is my hope that this handbook will serve three purposes: first to present the complete, official Mah Jong game to the beginner in such a way that an hour's reading will enable him to play it without difficulty; second, to refresh the memory of the player in America who is already familiar with one form of the game and wishes to reread the rules he knows; and third, to offer to non-Oriental players in the Orient a reference for their convenience in playing any of the varieties of the Oriental game.

Part One is devoted to the official game. The beginner will find it necessary only to read the first three chapters in order to be able to play to his satisfaction. *Chapter One* explains the meanings of the tiles; *Chapter Two* outlines the preliminaries, such as the deal; and *Chapter Three* presents the goal of the game and the playing procedure. The tables at the beginning of *Chapter Four* are all that it is necessary to use for scoring; the bulk of the chapter is then devoted to explanations and abundant examples covering all the possible scoring situations.

The text and drawings in *Part One* are explanatory or illustrative in nature, and a quick reading should make it evident that the number of actual rules is in fact very small. Furthermore, many sections are marked "optional," and can simply be skipped, to be read later when the player chooses.

Part Two covers all the alternatives, variations and additions to the game which are likely to be of interest to American players. The old hand will find it useful to read *Part One*, and then skim *Part Two* to find the additional rules with which he is familiar. Each chapter in *Part Two* is roughly parallel to the corresponding chapter of *Part One*. *Chapter One*, for example, explains the uses of extra tiles and accessories in the set which are no longer found in the official game, and Chapter Four covers the variations on scoring, including a brief explanation of "riichi." *Chapter Five* is an extra scoring chapter, giving tables for the strictly American scoring rules of the mixed-hand, one-double and cleared-hand games.

Part Three presents the fundamentals of strategy, which I hope will be useful to all Mah Jong players. It is written mainly for players of the official game, but notes are included where different tactics would be advisable in different games.

The terminology I have used is in accord, wherever possible, with that of *The American Code of Laws for Mah Jong* (copyright 1924 by the John H. Smith Publishing Corp.). It is entirely in English, and wherever new terms are introduced, they are given as the most reasonable English equivalents of the Japanese. The Glossary Index at the end of the book includes all the English terms, both mine and those of the American Code, and makes clear the few differences between them.

For those who wish to learn the Chinese or Japanese equivalents, these terms are also included.

My thanks to the many people who have been of assistance in the preparation of this book, and especially to Miss Fusako Takemasa and Mr. Kazuo Nagayama for their patient and generous help.

PART ONE

The Official Game

CHAPTER ONE

The Mah Jong Set

TILES

Individual sets vary, although the illustrations below will approximate any set the reader has. Some sets, made specially for export, have arabic numerals and letters (indicating the four winds) included on the tiles for the convenience of non-Oriental players. Learning the designations from the symbols and the Chinese characters is simple, however, and allows one more latitude in the purchase of his Mah Jong set.

The complete modern set consists of 136 tiles. These are divided into two groups, the *suits* and the *honors*, each group being further subdivided as indicated below. In addition to the 136 tiles, every set contains four extra blanks in case a tile should be damaged or lost, and some sets, especially those for export, contain other special tiles (flowers and seasons) which are no longer used in Japanese Mah Jong. See *Part Two, Chapter One.*

Suit Tiles

There are three suits, each consisting of thirty-six tiles: four 1's, four 2's, four 3's and so on up to 9. The names of these three suits are *bamboos, characters* and *dots*. There are four of each of the tiles depicted below.

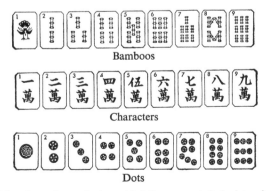

Bamboos

Characters

Dots

Note that the 1 bamboo, above, depicts a bird. In some sets it depicts a bamboo shoot.

In scoring, the 1's and 9's in the above groups are of higher value than the tiles 2 through 8. They should be thought of in a separate category, as the *terminals*. The tiles 2 through 8 are known as the *simples*.

Terminals

Honor Tiles

There are two types of honor tiles: the four *winds* (East, South, West, and North (and the three *dragons* (green, white, and red). There are four of each of these; thus, twenty-eight honors in all. One each of the honor tiles are depicted below.

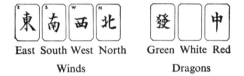

East South West North   Green White Red

Winds   Dragons

ACCESSORIES

Bones

In addition to the tiles, the complete Mah Jong set also contains a set of *bones* used, like the chips in poker, for scoring. In some American sets these have been replaced by chips with holes in the middle, which can be stacked on poles, but they will be called bones throughout this book. Each player receives the same number of bones at the beginning of the game. At the end of each hand the winner receives bones equal in value to his score from the loser(s). At the end of the game, the player with the highest count in bones is the winner.

There are usually four kinds of bones; the markings vary, but the most numerous ones should always be assigned the lowest value.

Bones

The Japan Mah Jong Association rules state that the bones should be valued at 500, 100 and 10. The one shown on the left should not be used. Each player receives two 500-point bones, nine 100-point bones, and ten 10-point bones at the beginning of the game, making a total of 2000 points.

Arbitrary values, however, may be assigned to them as the players choose. Many Japanese value them much higher, as described on page 78.

Dice

A pair of dice accompanies each set. These are used to determine the first dealer, and the starting point in the wall of each deal. They usually have rounded corners and the one-spot is often an uncolored hollow in the face of the die. A throw is considered valid only if both dice lie flat on top of the table within the wall. The dice are placed in front of the dealer during play, identifying which player is the dealer.

Discs

Discs are sometimes also found in the set, but are not necessary to the game. See page 21 for a description of their use.

CHAPTER TWO

Preliminaries

The distinction should be made clear between a *game* and a *hand* of Mah Jong. The complete game ordinarily consists of sixteen hands of play. Each hand begins with the building of the wall, breaking the wall, and dealing. Before the game, the players are seated in a random arrangement, and the dealer for the first hand is selected.

The American method of deciding the seating arrangement and dealer is recommended for those who wish to dispense with all but the essentials of the game. It is given on page 65. It involves only one throw of the dice and insures a random distribution of the players. The Japanese method (optional) involves four throws of the dice, and is officially sanctioned by the Mah Jong Association. It is given below.

BEFORE THE GAME

Seating Arrangement

Naming of Seats: First, the four players seat themselves arbitrarily. Then any player throws the dice, and beginning with himself as one, the player on his right as two, etc., he counts counter-clockwise to the number shown by the dice. The seat thus indicated is "temporary East," and the other three seats, in counterclockwise order, are temporary South, West and North. Contrary to expectations, the four winds do not seat the players according to the compass, but rather in the order that the four directions are customarily listed in Chinese.

EXAMPLE

1. Any player throws the dice. Here A throws a 6.

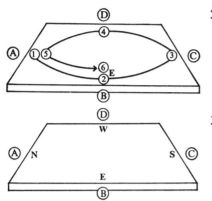

2. He counts up to six, counter-clockwise, starting with himself, to determine "temporary East."

3. The other seats are named accordingly.

Placing the Players: Now four wind tiles, one of each wind, are mixed face-down on the table and arranged in a row. If the set has discs, they may be used instead. At one end of the row an even-numbered suit tile is placed face up; at the other end, an odd-numbered suit tile.

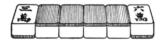

The player in the "temporary East" seat throws the dice and counts counterclockwise, beginning with himself, as before. The player indicated by the dice then picks up the wind tile at the odd end of the row if the number thrown was odd, or at the even end of the row, if the number was even. Each of the other players in order, counterclockwise, picks up a tile from the same end. The players then assume the seats indicated by the tiles they have drawn.

EXAMPLE

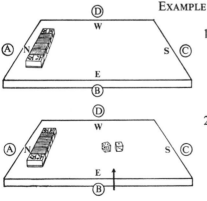

1. Any player (A in this case) arranges four wind tiles in a row, between an odd- and an even-numbered suit tile.

2. The player in the "temporary East" seat (B in this case) throws the dice. They show 3.

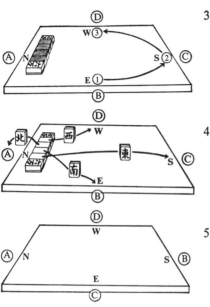

3. This indicates player D.

4. Player D picks up the wind tile at the odd end of the row; it is West. Player A picks up the next tile; it is North. B then draws South and C draws East.

5. The players then assume these seats.

Selecting the First Dealer

Now "temporary East" throws the dice and counts counterclockwise, beginning with himself, to the number shown. The player thus indicated casts the dice again, and again counts to the total. The player indicated by the *second* casting of the dice is now *dealer;* the other three players are the *non-dealers.*

The seat names now no longer apply. The dealer is East, and the other players are named in order, South, West and North.

EXAMPLE

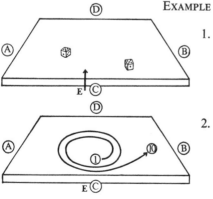

1. "Temporary East" (C) throws the dice. They show 10.

2. 10 indicates player B.

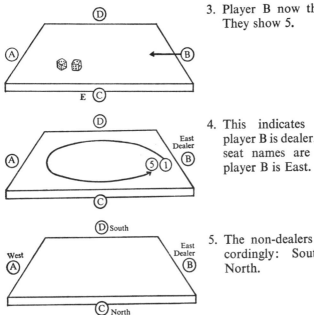

3. Player B now throws the dice. They show 5.

4. This indicates himself. Thus player B is dealer. The temporary seat names are now dropped; player B is East.

5. The non-dealers are named accordingly: South, West and North.

The bones should be distributed now, according to the following:

Value	Number dealt to each player	Initial points given to each player
10	10	100
100	9	900
500	2	1000
	total	2000

BEFORE EACH HAND

Building the Wall

The 136 tiles are now well mixed in the middle of the table. Be sure to *exclude* the extra four blanks and the flower and season tiles, if there are any. Traditionally this is done with a tremendous clatter, all four players plunging in with both hands. The table should be covered with a soft cloth or blanket to eliminate excess noise. Each player then gathers thirty-four tiles and builds a row seventeen long and two high in front of him.

Note: Officially, the tiles should all be kept face-down during this procedure. In an informal game, however, no attempt is made to conceal them.

The Japanese love of precision and ceremony has given rise to a standard method of stacking the tiles. This optional procedure is as follows: first pick up three tiles, face down, in each hand and place in a row; then pick up three more in each hand and add to the row at each end; then pick up two in one hand and three in the other, and add at each end.

This automatically secures a row of 17 tiles. Finally, repeat the process, making another row, and lift the second, grasped firmly at each end, all at once onto the first.

Each player then pushes his row forward. When the wall is built, it will meet at all four corners. To move a row, grasp it firmly at each end, pressing toward the middle. Slide it right and left and right again, gradually moving forward.

The arrangement then is as illustrated. Each pile of two tiles is called a *stack*.

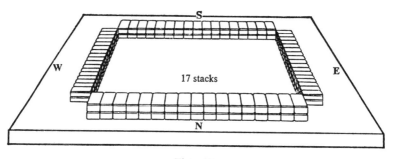

The wall

Breaking the Wall

First, the dealer casts the dice and counts counterclockwise, beginning with himself, to the number shown. The deal usually will begin somewhere in the row of tiles in front of the indicated player. This player casts the dice again and adds the numbers shown by the *two* castings of the dice. He then counts off that number of stacks, beginning with the right end of the row in front of him and counting towards his left. If the grand total exceeds 17, the count of stacks continues around the corner to the row in front of the player at his left. He makes a break in the wall after the stack at which the count ended, and the deal begins with the stack to the left of the break.

For a slightly simpler method of breaking the wall, and for the custom of establishing a pair of "loose tiles," see page 65.

EXAMPLE

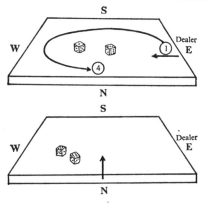

1. The dealer throws the dice. They show 4, which is North.

2. North throws the dice. They show 10. The two numbers added are 14.

3. North then separates 14 stacks from the right end of his row of tiles. The deal begins with the 15th stack.

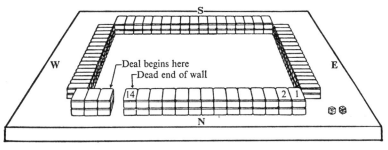

Breaking the wall after stack 14

Suppose the two castings of the dice added up to more than 17. North would count off his 17 stacks and continue counting along the row in front of West until the total number of the two castings of the dice is counted off.

The Deal

East picks up four tiles (two stacks) from the left of the break and each of the other players in order (South, West, North) follows suit, repeating this three times, so that each player has twelve tiles. East now picks up two to make a hand of fourteen, and the other players in turn then pick up one tile each as indicated, giving each of them a total of thirteen.

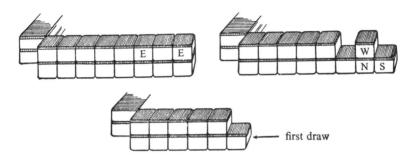

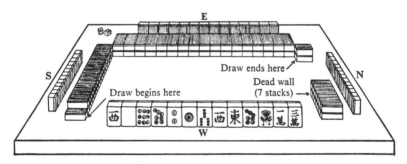

first draw

The Japanese call this procedure *chan-chan* because of the sound made by the clicking of the two tiles East picks up, and the players are quick to remind the dealer to go *chan-chan* when the time comes.

Finally, seven stacks are set aside from the far end of the wall. These, the *dead wall*, are not touched except in the case of a four, described below. If no one can go out by the time the wall is exhausted, excluding these last fourteen tiles, the hand is a draw.

Each player arranges his tiles in a row facing himself, and East, who has one more tile than the others, will begin the play by discarding a tile.

Draw ends here

Dead wall
(7 stacks) →

Draw begins here

The playing arrangement

CHAPTER THREE

Playing

THE GOAL OF MAH JONG

The goal of the game is to "go out" by completing a hand composed of four *sets* of three tiles each, plus a *pair*, thus totaling fourteen tiles. A set may also be composed of four tiles, the total of fourteen being increased by one for each such set. When one goes out, he does not discard, hence he has the necessary fourteen tiles. A set may be any of the following:

> a *sequence* (three consecutive tiles of one suit)
> a *triplet* (three identical tiles), or
> a *four* (four identical tiles).

The *pair* may be any two identical tiles.

REGULAR PLAYING PROCEDURE

East begins the hand by discarding a tile; he places it in front of him face up. Play proceeds to East's right, each player in turn drawing one tile from the wall and discarding one by placing it face up in front of him. Each player's discards are kept separate from the others', and are placed in order, from left to right, so that the other players can easily see what kind of tiles have been discarded, and in what order.

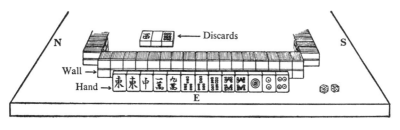

Discards

Optional: It is the convention, when playing Mah Jong, for each player to name his discard for the convenience of his opponents. East discards, for example, and announces "red dragon." South then draws and discards, announcing "1 character," and so on. In practice, however, this is seldom done.

Ordinarily, the players follow in order, drawing and discarding as described, but if one wishes to use a discarded tile, and can complete a set by doing so, he may declare, as explained below.

"CHOW"—MAKING A SEQUENCE

If you have two of the three members necessary to make a sequence, and *the player on your left* discards the missing member, then you may declare "chow" and claim the discarded tile instead of drawing from the wall. You must then *meld* by displaying face-up on your right the two tiles from your hand which form part of the sequence, adding the claimed tile to them, and then discard. For a faster method of chowing see page 67.

You may declare "chow" only when it is your turn, and may pick up only the *last* tile discarded by the player on your left.

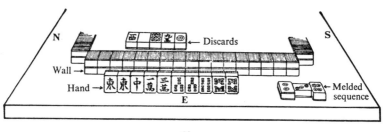

Chow

There are optional penalties for melding incorrectly, or failing to meld after declaring "chow," which are described at the end of this chapter.

Optional: It is the convention when melding a sequence to place the tile you obtained from the player on your left at right angles to the other two, so that everyone may see which one he discarded.

"PUNG"—MAKING A TRIPLET

Triplets are often naturally accumulated in the hand through drawing all three members from the wall. They may then stay concealed throughout the game.

If you have a pair in your hand and *any* player discards an identical tile, you may declare "pung" and claim the discarded tile instead of drawing from the wall. The convention is the same as with "chow"; you should first meld the pair from your hand, add the claimed tile, and then discard. For a faster method of punging, see page 67.

You may declare "pung" only immediately after the tile you want is discarded. The play then continues to *your* right, skipping anyone between you and the player who discarded the tile.

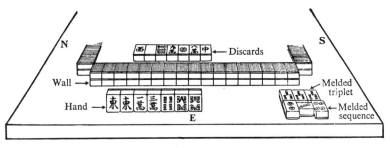

Pung

There are optional penalties for melding incorrectly, or failing to meld after declaring "pung," which are described at the end of this chapter.

The diagrams below illustrate the difference between "chow" and "pung." You may declare "chow" only for a tile discarded by the player on your left. This does not interrupt the normal order of play. You may declare "pung" for any discarded tile, and after your turn, play proceeds to your right. This sometimes does interrupt the normal order of play.

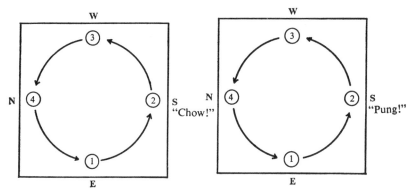

1. E discards.
2. S says "chow," melds, and discards.
3. W continues, followed by
4. N.

1. E discards.
2. S says "pung," melds, and discards.
3. W continues, followed by
4. N.

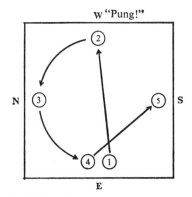

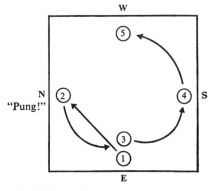

1. E discards.	1. E discards.
2. W says "pung," melds, and discards.	2. N says "pung," melds, and discards.
3. N continues, followed by	3. E plays again, followed by
4. E and finally	4. S and finally
5. S.	5. W.

"KONG"—MAKING A FOUR

There are three ways to make a four: first, from a triplet in your hand and a discarded tile; second, from a triplet in your hand and a tile drawn from the wall; and third, from a melded triplet and a drawn tile. You cannot make a four from a melded triplet and a discarded tile, because no set may include more than one discarded tile.

Triplet Plus Discard

If you have been dealt a triplet or have received one by drawing, and any player discards the fourth, you may declare "kong" and claim the discarded tile. Melding your triplet and adding the claimed tile to it and then discarding would leave you with one less tile in your hand than you should have. In the case of a kong, you must also draw a tile from the *dead* wall to make up this deficit. This is called a *supplement tile*. After drawing this tile you then discard.

You may declare "kong" only immediately after the tile you want is discarded. The play then continues to your right, skipping anyone between you and the player who discarded your tile, as with "pung," above.

There are optional penalties for melding incorrectly, or failing to meld after declaring "kong." These are explained at the end of this chapter.

In all three cases mentioned above, "chow," "pung" and "kong," you may take only the last discarded tile. Tiles previously discarded are irrecoverable.

Triplet Plus Draw

If you have a triplet in your hand and draw the fourth from the wall, you may make a *concealed four*. Declare "kong," display your four, draw a supplement tile from the dead wall, and discard. You should place your four with the two tiles in the center face up and the end two face down. This indicates a concealed four.

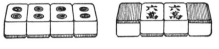

Melded four   Concealed four

Melded Triplet Plus Draw

If you have a melded triplet and draw the fourth from the wall, you may declare "kong" and add it to your triplet to make a melded four. You then draw a supplement tile from the dead wall and discard as usual.

Robbing a Kong: If you need only one tile to go out, and someone else makes a melded four with that tile by drawing from the wall to a melded triplet, you may go "out" by taking the tile from his four. For the ordinary method of going out see below.

"OUT"

When you need only one tile to go out, your hand is *ready*. For the "ready" declaration, see page 71. Now you may discover that some tile you have previously discarded would permit you to go out. This tile is called a *sacred discard*. If another player discards an identical tile, you may not use it unless you have drawn from the wall at least once subsequent to your own discard. For other sacred discard rules, see page 72.

Barring this case, when another player discards the tile that completes your hand, you may declare "out" and take the discarded tile. Or if you draw the tile that completes your hand you may declare "out." You then display your hand and the score is calculated.

There is a penalty for declaring "out" mistakenly. For this see the end of this chapter.

Precedence of Declarations

Of the four declarations, "chow," "pung," "kong" and "out," "chow" is the least powerful, "pung" and "kong" next, and "out" is the most powerful. Thus, if two players want the same tile, one for a sequence and the other for a triplet or four, the player who declares "pung" or "kong" gets the tile.

It is impossible for two players to declare "chow" simultaneously, because one may only declare "chow" for a tile discarded by the player on one's left. It is also impossible for two players to declare "pung" or "kong" simultaneously, because there are only four tiles of each kind in the set. Thus when a desired tile is discarded, two players cannot both be holding identical pairs or triplets in their hands.

If two or three players declare "out" for the same discarded tile, the player who would have played first may take it. However, after a player has claimed a tile and *discarded*, the tile is his. The act of discarding completes his turn, and no one may take the tile from him, even to go out. For the draw rule, which is no longer in force, see page 69.

Displaying the Hand (Optional)

For convenience in scoring, the Japanese use a special system of displaying the hand to distinguish more from less valuable sets. This system is given in full on page 68.

DRAW

If no one has gone out by the time the wall is exhausted, a *draw* is declared. The hand stops, the deal passes, and a new hand begins. If any supplement tiles have been drawn from the dead wall, the drawing must stop that many tiles sooner, i.e., at the end of a hand there must be fourteen tiles remaining on the table. Theoretically this would be the dead wall, but in the case of fours, where supplement tiles have been drawn, the dead wall has been depleted. In this case the hand must stop with that many tiles remaining in the "live" wall so that the total number of remaining tiles will add up to fourteen.

In popular play, many other draw rules are added to this one, some of which are noted on page 69.

DEALER'S EXTRA HAND

If East wins, he retains the deal, and the hand is called a dealer's extra hand and is played in addition to the sixteen hands of a game. There is no limit to the number of extra hands the dealer may play. Popularly, bonuses are given for extra hands, and special rules are applied, as described on page 70, but these are not allowed by the Japan Mah Jong Association.

THE COMPLETE GAME

At the end of the hand, the score is calculated, and the losers pay the winner his score in bones. The deal then passes to the right, unless East has won. The new dealer assumes the name East and retains the dice as a marker, and the other players accordingly have new winds.

One *round* is completed when each of the four players has held and lost the deal. One complete *game* consists of four such rounds. The first round is the "East round" and the East wind is said to *prevail*. The second round is the "South round," the third is "West," and the fourth, "North." Each player deals once (and if he wins, more than once) in each round.

When a player's *own wind* coincides with the *prevailing wind*, it is called his *double wind*, and is of special value to him. Each player has a double wind once in each round. See diagram on page 148.

A complete game, when played by experts, lasts about one and a half hours. Thus, several can be played in a single session. For beginners, however, the game may last as long as three or four hours.

PENALTIES (OPTIONAL)

The following penalties are seldom used by Japanese players of Mah Jong except in tournament play. The only one used frequently in informal games is the 100-point penalty imposed for declaring "chow," "pung" or "kong" incorrectly as in the third instance cited below. This is the only one I have found to be important.

"Out": If a player declares "out," and is found to have done so mistakenly or illegally and any of the other players display their hands, the hand ends. If the score limit is 500, the offender, if a non-dealer, must pay 250 to each of the other non-dealers and 500 to the dealer, the total penalty amounting to 1000. If the dealer is the offender, he must pay 500 to each of the other players, the total amounting to 1500.

If no other player's hand is displayed at the time of such a false "out," the hand continues and the offender is penalized by not being permitted to go out until after his next turn.

Long Hand; Short Hand; Foul Hand; Intentional Display: If at any time during the game a player is found to have, for any reason at all, either more or less than thirteen tiles, plus one for each "four" in his hand, the player may not go out. He serves for the rest of the hand simply as a dead weight, continuing in the play simply in order to complete the hand, during which his only objective is to cause a draw.

Similarly, if a player melds an incorrect sequence, triplet, or four, and the next player has begun his turn, the melded set must be left as it stands, and the offender prohibited from going out. If the error is corrected before the next player has begun his turn no penalty is involved.

If a player intentionally displays part or all of his own or any other hand, he may not go out.

In all of the above cases, the offender must continue to draw and discard in order to enable his opponents to continue playing. His only remaining objective, as noted above, is to cause a draw.

Changing of Mind or Failure to Meld after "Chow," "Pung" or "Kong": If a player declares "chow," "pung," or "kong," and then finds that he cannot meld his set, or fails to meld his set, or changes his mind and draws from the wall, he must forfeit 100 points, which are placed in the center of the table and collected by the player who wins the hand that is in progress. In the event of a draw, or if the offender himself wins the hand, he reclaims the penalty.

Mistaken Discard: If a player discards a tile mistakenly, he may not reclaim it.

Missed Discard: If a player fails to claim the tile which would complete his hand when it is discarded, he may not go out on any subsequent discard of that tile until after his next draw from the wall. For example: you are East, waiting for 5 character. South discards 5 character and you fail to notice it. Then West discards another 5 character. You may not go out by claiming this second 5 character discard. In your next turn you draw and discard. Then, supposing West again discards a 5 character, you may use it to go out.

Other Provisions: If a player is responsible in any other way, except as noted above, for making the continuation of a fair game impossible, the hand stops, and he must pay the same penalty described above in the paragraph headed *"Out."*

If a player departs in any less serious way from the rules, the hand continues, and the players must agree on a penalty, or a judge must arbitrate.

Insurance Penalties: See page 75.

ETIQUETTE (OPTIONAL)

The following rules of etiquette are suggested by the Japan Mah Jong Association. Some of them differ from the procedures in popular use, notably those that deal with slips of the hand in playing. In an informal game, there is no need to keep the tiles face-down during mixing, or to build the wall according to the exact prescription, but in formal competition players should abide by these rules.

1. The tiles shall be placed face down on the table before mixing, and shall be mixed thoroughly. If any lucky tiles turn over during the process, the mixing continues until the location of the tiles is unknown to all players.

2. The rows in front of each player, which form the wall, shall consist of exactly seventeen stacks each.

3. The dice shall be thrown within the wall, and a throw shall be considered valid only when both dice lie flat within the wall.

4. Discards shall be placed quietly on the table.

5. The discards of each player shall be arranged in one or two orderly rows within the wall, in front of him.

6. Each player shall await his turn to draw. Drawing before the player on the left has discarded, and feeling the face of the tile while it is held face-down in the hand before the turn, is not permitted.

7. If "chow," "pung" or "kong" is declared mistakenly, the player must explain his mistake. If subsequent to saying "chow," "pung" or "kong," a player changes his mind and decides to draw from the wall, he must display the tiles of his hand which would have formed part of his melded set.

8. When "chow," "pung" or "kong" is declared, the player shall not discard until after he has melded.

9. Players shall not discuss discards.

10. Players shall not talk about their own or their opponents' hands.

11. Players shall not attempt to rattle their opponents by talking.

12. Scoring shall be speedy. No mistakes made in scoring may be corrected after the dice have been thrown for the next deal.

13. Non-players shall not make comments about the game.

14. Players shall not display their pleasure at good luck or their disappointment at bad luck.

15. If, while the wall is being built, a tile is exposed so that the players know its location, the row in which the tile appears shall be re-mixed and rebuilt.

16. If during play a player exposes the tile he would have drawn, he shall take it.

17. If during play any other tile of the wall is accidentally exposed, it shall be mixed with six adjacent stacks (or as many as are available), and that portion of the wall rebuilt.

CHAPTER FOUR

Scoring

The following summary and scoring table include all the essential rules of scoring. However, playing the game brings out complexities that are not immediately apparent from reading the table. For this reason most of the remainder of the chapter is devoted to definitions, further explanations, and liberal use of illustrations showing all the possible types of hands. These are all listed under the same headings used in the scoring table.

The scoring rules presented in this chapter are in complete accord with those of the Japan Mah Jong Association. Other rules, used popularly, increase the value of certain hands and supplement the official system with bonuses for special inclusions in the hand which are not officially given any credit. These are explained in *Part Two, Chapter Four*, starting on page 78.

At the end of the present chapter are instructions as to how the winner should be paid, how penalties are collected, and so forth. Alternatives and popular additions to this section will also be found in *Part Two, Chapter Four*, starting on page 89.

Note: In the illustrations for the following examples, "C" below a set means "concealed"; "M" means "melded." Dots on the faces of the tiles simply indicate the other tiles are assumed to be in the hand.

SCORING PROCEDURE IN GENERAL

The beginner will find scoring difficult unless he makes a few clear distinctions from the beginning. It is basically a three-step process involving points, doubles, and payment. Each step must be completed before the next is begun.

When a hand is won, the winner displays his hand and scores it. He is responsible for exhibiting its full value. If he fails to score it properly, the other players may correct him. Once he has been paid and the dice have been thrown for the next hand, however, the score must stand even if incorrect. A brief elucidation of the three steps in scoring follows. Each is explained more fully later in this chapter.

Points: Twenty points are given as a reward for winning the hand. Each set in the hand is then credited with points if it merits them, and these are added to the initial 20. If the last tile of the hand was drawn from the wall, an additional 2 points are given and if the last tile completed the hand by fitting into the only possible "one-chance" place, 2 more points are added. If the hand was concealed throughout but went out with a discarded tile, it is given 10 points more. These points are not interdependent, and all those that fit the hand are added to determine the *total points* earned.

Doubles: The point score having been decided, the winner shows the ways, if any, in which his hand is worthy of doubles. I have divided the doubles into seven categories. Beginners would do well to examine the hand from each of the seven points of view involved and systematically check to see what doubles it has earned. The hand may be viewed in any ways the winner chooses, and all doubles that apply may be given. As in the case of points, they are not interdependent.

If the hand earns one double, the total points are multiplied by 2. If it earns two doubles, the total points are multiplied by 2×2, or 4. If it earns three doubles, the multiplying factor is $2 \times 2 \times 2$, or 8. If four, by 16; if five, by 32, etc.

Let us say that the *total points* of the winner's hand came to $20 + 2 + 2 + 16 + 2$, or 42, and that it had three doubles. The point score of 42 is multiplied by $2 \times 2 \times 2$, or 8, yielding 336. This is the *total score* of the hand and is the basis upon which the winner must be paid.

Payment: As outlined on page 18, the players each have 2000 points' worth of bones at the start of the game. Since the lowest denomination in bones is 10, the winner's score must be rounded off to the nearest 10 before he can be paid. In the example, 336 is rounded off to 340. This is the winner's *final score.*

The player who was responsible for the winner's going out, that is the player whose discarded tile completed the winner's hand, must pay. Occasionally, of course, the winner goes out on a tile drawn from the wall, in which case no single opponent is responsible. In this case all three losers must pay. The dealer must always pay or be paid double.

There are in all four possible payment situations: 1) If the dealer goes out self-drawn, each player pays him double the final score. 2) If the dealer goes out on a discard, the discarder pays him six times the final score. 3) If a non-dealer goes out on a drawn tile, the dealer pays him double the final score and each of the other losers pays him the final score without doubling. · 4) If a non-dealer goes out on a discard, the discarder, whether dealer or not, pays him four times his score.

The payment is transacted in bones. Let us say that the winner in our example was not the dealer, and that he went out on a tile drawn from the wall. The dealer pays him 2 times 340, or 680, and each of the other losers pays him 340. Thus he receives a total of 1360 in bones.

If any penalties have been placed in the middle of the table during the hand, the winner collects them at this time.

The chart and the scoring outline below may be of some use to beginners.

INITIAL POINTS AND THE LIMIT

When hands are scored, their values sometimes reach exceedingly high levels, while the number of bones the players have is strictly limited. Based on the official valuing and distribution of the bones at the start, a maximum score of 500 points must be imposed. This maximum score, the *limit*, is the highest *final score* with which a player may be credited before payment. Since he is paid by each player and paid double by the dealer, or if he is the dealer he is paid double by each player, he then can receive a maximum of 2000 if a non-dealer, or 3000 if dealer.

In addition to making the limit by virtue of exceeding 500 in final score, a player may make certain kinds of hands which automatically, without calculation, receive the limit. Ten such hands are described on pages 56-59.

SCORING OUTLINE

Points

For winning	20
The hand	
Set 1	
Set 2	
Set 3	
Set 4	
Pair	
Last tile	
Self-drawn (2 points)	
One-chance (2 points)	
If this total is 20, see *no-points* on page 50....................	
Concealed hand with discarded tile (10 points)	
TOTAL POINTS	

Doubles

For 1 double multiply total points by   2
  „   2 doubles   „   „   „   „   4
  „   3   „   „   „   „   „   8
  „   4   „   „   „   „   „   16
  „   5   „   „   „   „   „   32

TOTAL SCORE (Not to exceed 500) ....

FINAL SCORE (Total score rounded out to nearest 10) ....

SCORING TABLE

POINTS

Winning 20

Sets

Sequences 0

Melded triplets
Simples 2
Terminals or honors 4

Concealed triplets
Simples 4
Terminals or honors 8

Melded fours
Simples 8
Terminals or honors 16

Concealed fours
Simples 16
Terminals or honors 32

Pairs
Suit tiles 0
Ordinary winds 0
Lucky tiles 2
Double wind 4

Last Tile of Hand
Discarded 0
Self-drawn 2
One-chance 2

Concealed Hand
With discarded tile 10
With self-drawn tile (see *Doubles*, below.)

DOUBLES

Lucky Sets
Lucky triplet or four 1
Double wind triplet or four .. 2

Concealed Hand
With discarded tile (10 points)
With self-drawn tile 1

Groups of Sets
Four triplets, including fours
0, 1 or 2 concealed 1
3 concealed 2
4 concealed .... limit
Three concealed triplets with
one sequence 1

Ways of Going Out
Last tile of wall 1
Last discarded tile.......... 1
Robbing a kong 1
Supplement tile 1

Special Inclusions
Three consecutive sequences .. 1

No-points 1

Consistency
All simples 1
All terminals and honors 1
Terminal or honor in each set.. 1
One suit with honors 1
One suit only 4
Little three dragons 1

LIMIT HANDS

Big three dragons
Little four winds
Big four winds
All honors
All terminals

Four concealed triplets
Heavenly hand
Earthly hand
Nine gates
Thirteen orphans

PAYMENT

	Multiple of final score to be paid		
	By discarder	By each player	By dealer
If dealer goes out self-drawn	—	2	—
If dealer goes out on a discard	6	—	—
If non-dealer goes out self-drawn	—	1	2
If non-dealer goes out on a discard	4	—	—

The winner also collects all penalties on the table.

POINTS

Points for Winning

The player who goes out wins the hand. He receives 20 points automatically, as the basic score of his hand.

For winning **20**

Points for Sets

Each of the sets in his hand is examined and credited with points. A sequence is valueless as a set, though it may be useful for acquiring doubles.

Sequence **0**

Triplets and fours are divided into 1) *simples* and 2) *terminals and honors* and are valued according to whether they have been melded or concealed. A *concealed set* is defined as a set all of whose tiles were drawn from the wall. A *melded set* includes one discarded tile. Thus, if a player went out on a discarded tile, the set completed by that tile is considered melded.

Melded triplets
    Simples **2**
    Terminals or honors **4**
Concealed triplets
    Simples **4**
    Terminals or honors **8**
Melded fours
    Simples **8**
    Terminals or honors **16**
Concealed fours
    Simples **16**
    Terminals or honors **32**

Pairs are valued differently. They are worth nothing unless composed of *lucky tiles:* the three dragons, the prevailing wind, and the player's own wind. This excludes the two wind tiles that are neither prevailing nor one's own.

Lucky tiles
Red dragon
White dragon
Green dragon
Prevailing wind
Own wind

A pair of lucky tiles is worth 2 points. If it is a double wind pair (for example, you are South in the South round, and you make a pair of South), it is worth 4 points. It makes no difference whether the pair is concealed or melded. These terms are never applied to pairs.

Pairs

Suit tiles	**0**
Ordinary winds	**0**
Prevailing wind	**2**
Own wind	**2**
Dragons	**2**
Double wind	**4**

Points for Last Tile of Hand

Two main factors are considered in calculating these points: first, whether the last tile was drawn from the wall or was claimed from someone else's discard; and secondly, the use to which the last tile was put in completing a sequence, a triplet, or the pair.

You receive no points *per se* for going out with a discarded tile. For going out *self-drawn*, by drawing a tile from the wall, you receive 2 points.

Discarded Tile	**0**
Self-drawn	**2**

This last tile may, of course, complete a pair, a triplet, or a sequence and should be scored accordingly. In the case where there is only one possible use for the last tile, i.e., where there is only one opening, it merits 2 points as a *one-chance* "out." The reasoning behind this is that it is harder to get the one-chance tile than to get one of *several* needed tiles.

The following ready hands are the only kinds of one-chance hands possible. Each merits 2 points.

Waiting for the Pair: The ready hand has four complete sets and an isolated tile. It goes out on a tile that matches the isolated one.

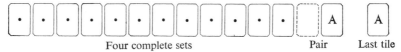

| Four complete sets | Pair | Last tile |

Waiting for Middle of Sequence: The ready hand has three complete sets and a pair and lacks the middle tile of a sequence. It goes out on the tile that completes the sequence.

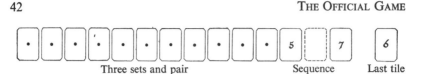

Three sets and pair   Sequence   Last tile

Waiting for End of Sequence: The ready hand has three complete sets and a pair, and lacks the inside tile of a terminal sequence (either the 3 of a 1-2-3 sequence or the 7 of a 7-8-9 sequence). It goes out on the tile that completes the sequence.

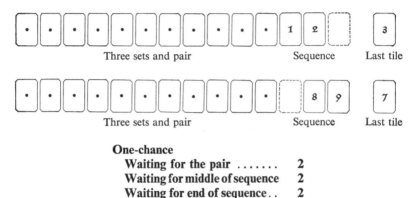

Three sets and pair   Sequence   Last tile

Three sets and pair   Sequence   Last tile

One-chance
Waiting for the pair **2**
Waiting for middle of sequence   **2**
Waiting for end of sequence..   **2**

Note: Combining the above rules, if you both draw the last tile and complete a one-chance hand with it, you get 4 points.

Freedom of Count: A player who has two or more alternative ways of scoring the last tile of his hand may pick the way which gives him the higher final score. For example, if the ready hand contained 2-3-4-4, and the last tile of the hand is a 4, the player may display it as having completed the pair, and get 2 points, or as having completed the sequence, and get 0 points. The latter may be advantageous if the hand otherwise qualifies as a no-points hand, as described on page 50.

Points for Concealed Hand

In a concealed hand, every tile has been drawn from the wall. To be completely concealed, this hand should also go out on a tile drawn from the wall. However, it deserves some credit for being concealed, even if it goes out on a discarded tile. To make the scoring fair, the hand is given ten points if it goes out with a discarded tile, but multiplied by two if it goes out self-drawn. See *Doubles*, on page 46.

Concealed hand
With discarded tile **10**
Self-drawn (see *Doubles*)

Point-Counting Examples

The following are not complete scoring examples: they do not illustrate doubles or final calculation of payment, but only the actual points for the situations described up to now. After totaling the points, the winner must multiply for doubles as explained in the following section.

EXAMPLE 1: Concealed hand containing no melded sets till final turn. Discarded tile was 2 bamboo. East round; player is West.

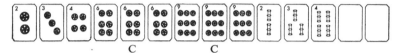

$$20 + 0 + 4 + 8 + 0 + 2 + 10 = 44$$

20 for winning; 0 for sequence; 4 for concealed triplet of simples; 8 for concealed triplet of terminals; 0 for sequence; 2 for lucky pair; 10 for concealed hand with discarded tile.

EXAMPLE 2: Concealed hand containing no melded sets. Self-drawn tile was 3 bamboo. West round; player is North.

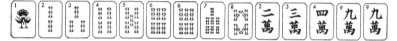

$$(20 + 0 + 0 + 0 + 0 + 0 + 2 + 2) \times 2 = 48$$

20 for winning; 0 for each sequence; 0 for pair, because 9's are not lucky tiles; 2 for one-chance hand; 2 for self-drawn tile. Total multiplied by 2 for concealed self-drawn hand.

EXAMPLE 3: Partially melded hand in which one or more sets have been melded. Self-drawn tile was 4 character. South round; player is East.

$$20 + 0 + 0 + 8 + 4 + 2 + 2 = 36$$

20 for winning; 0 for each sequence; 8 for concealed triplet of honors; 4 for melded triplet of honors; 2 for pair because South is the prevailing wind; 2 for self-drawn tile.

EXAMPLE 4: Partially melded hand. Discarded tile was 8 character. West round; player is West.

$$20 + 0 + 4 + 4 + 2 + 4 + 2 = 36$$

20 for winning; 0 for sequence; 4 for melded triplet of terminals; 4 for melded triplet of honors; 2 for melded triplet of simples; 4 for double-wind pair; 2 for one-chance hand.

EXAMPLE 5: Partially melded hand. Discarded tile was South. South round; player is South.

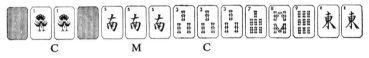

$$20 + 32 + 4 + 4 + 0 + 0 = 60$$

20 for winning; 32 for concealed four of terminals; 4 for melded triplet of honors; 4 for concealed triplet of simples; 0 for sequence; 0 for pair, because East is not a lucky tile.

EXAMPLE 6: Partially melded hand. Discarded tile was South. North round; player is West.

$$20 + 8 + 16 + 4 + 4 + 2 = 54$$

20 for winning; 8 for melded four of simples; 16 for melded four of honors; 4 for melded triplet of honors; 4 for melded triplet of honors; 2 for pair because West is the player's own wind.

Note: Players already familiar with the doubles, explained below, may wish to know the final scores in these examples. Example 1 hand receives no doubles. Example 2 hand receives one double for concealed self-drawn. Example 3 hand receives three doubles: two lucky sets and one suit with honors. Example 4 hand receives no doubles. Example 5 hand receives three doubles: double-wind set and one suit with honors. Example 6 hand receives four doubles: two lucky sets, four triplets, and one suit with honors.

DOUBLES

After adding up the points in the hand, you determine the number of *doubles*. If there is one double, the previously arrived at point total is multiplied by two; if two doubles, by four; if three doubles, by eight; if four, by sixteen, and so on, doubling the figure each time. You will readily see that a good hand is one that earns several doubles, rather than one whose point-count is high, though often the two go together.

A hand may receive doubles for certain kinds of triplets or fours, for containing certain patterns of tiles, for going out in certain ways, and for other conditions listed below.

Note: Many of the following doubles can be applied simultaneously to a single hand. It sometimes becomes difficult to keep track of all the scoring rules applicable to a single hand and therefore *it is incumbent upon the owner of the winning hand to score it properly.* If he underscores it, no one need call his attention to the fact. If he overscores it, he may be corrected by any other player. In any event, if a mistake is made, it may be corrected *only prior to the throw of the dice for the next hand.* After that, the score and payment stand, and no changes may be made.

Except where otherwise noted, the hand may be viewed in as many ways as possible, in order to secure the maximum number of doubles. Melded sets may not be rearranged, however, and all sets, both concealed and melded, must remain integral, as first displayed. The winner must first arrange, and then display his hand.

Doubles for Lucky Sets

Lucky sets are triplets or fours of lucky tiles. As explained above, the lucky tiles include the three dragons, the prevailing wind, and, for each player, his own wind. Each triplet or four of lucky tiles is worth one double for the whole hand, whether the set is melded or concealed. A double-wind triplet or four is worth two doubles.

Lucky triplet or four **1**
Double-wind triplet or four **2**

EXAMPLE 7: Partially melded hand. Self-drawn tile was South. West round; player is South.

$$(20 + 0 + 0 + 2 + 4 + 2 + 2) \times 2 = 60$$

Non-dealers pay 60; dealer pays 120

20 for winning; 0 for sequence; 0 for sequence; 2 for melded triplet of simples; 4 for melded triplet of honors; 2 for lucky pair; 2 for self-drawn tile. One double for the triplet of South, because it is the player's own wind.

Double for Concealed Self-Drawn Hand

As explained above, a concealed hand consists of tiles drawn only from the wall. If it goes out with a drawn tile as well, it receives one double. If it goes out with a discarded tile it receives instead 10 points, which is usually worth about one-half a double.

Note: A hand that goes out self-drawn always receives 2 points, regardless of whether it is concealed or not.

> **Partially melded hand**
> Discarded tile . . . .   **0 points, 0 double**
> Self-drawn tile . . . .**2 points, 0 double**
> **Concealed hand**
> Discarded tile . . . .   **10 points, 0 double**
> Self-drawn tile . . . .   **2 points, 1 double**

EXAMPLE 8: Concealed hand. Discarded tile, by dealer, was 3 bamboo. North round; player is West.

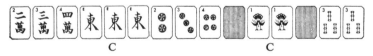

$$20 + 0 + 8 + 0 + 32 + 0 + 2 + 10 = 72$$

Dealer pays 4 × 70 to West

20 for winning; 0 for sequence; 8 for concealed triplet of honors; 0 for sequence; 32 for concealed four of terminals; 0 for pair; 2 for one-chance. Plus 10 for concealed hand with discarded tile.

EXAMPLE 9: Partially melded hand. Self-drawn tile was 3 bamboo. North round; player is West.

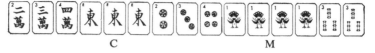

$$20 + 0 + 8 + 0 + 16 + 0 + 2 + 2 = 48$$

Non-dealers pay 50; dealer pays 100

20 for winning; 0 for sequence; 8 for concealed triplet of honors; 0 for sequence; 16 for melded four of terminals; 0 for pair; 2 for one-chance; 2 for self-drawn tile.

EXAMPLE 10: Concealed hand. Self-drawn tile was 3 bamboo. North round; player is West.

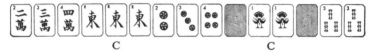

$$(20 + 0 + 8 + 0 + 32 + 0 + 2 + 2) \times 2 = 128$$

Non-dealers pay 130; dealer pays 260

20 for winning; 0 for sequence; 8 for concealed triplet of honors; 0 for sequence; 32 for concealed four of terminals; 0 for pair; 2 for one-chance; 2 for self-drawn tile. One double for concealed self-drawn hand.

Doubles for Groups of Sets

Four Triplets: A hand containing four triplets merits at least one double. If three of them are concealed, it is worth two doubles. If all four are concealed, it scores the limit. Fours can be counted as triplets in these hands.

Four triplets (including fours)	
0, 1 or 2 concealed	1
3 concealed	2
4 concealed	limit

EXAMPLE 11: Partially melded hand. Discarded tile, by South, was 3 dot. South round; player is West.

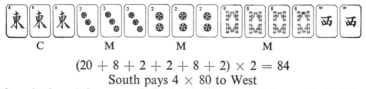

$$(20 + 8 + 2 + 2 + 8 + 2) \times 2 = 84$$

South pays 4 × 80 to West

20 for winning; 8 for concealed triplet of honors; 2 for melded triplet of simples; 2 for melded triplet of simples; 8 for melded four of simples; 2 for

lucky pair, because West is the player's own wind. One double for four triplets.

Three Concealed Triplets: A hand that does not have four triplets, but contains three concealed triplets, is worth one double. The fourth set in this hand is a sequence.

Three concealed triplets
with one sequence **1**

EXAMPLE 12: Concealed hand. Discarded tile, by North, was 9 character. East round; dealer.

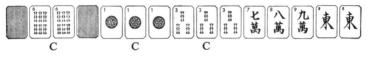

$(20 + 16 + 8 + 4 + 0 + 4 + 10) \times 2 = 124$
North pays 6×120 to dealer

20 for winning; 16 for concealed four of simples; 8 for concealed triplet of terminals; 4 for concealed triplet of simples; 0 for sequence; 4 for double-wind pair; 10 for concealed hand with discarded tile. One double for three concealed triplets.

Doubles for Ways of Going Out

Last Tile of Wall: If you go out with the very last tile in the wall, excluding the dead wall which originally had fourteen tiles and which may not be used for regular draws, you receive one double.

Going out with last tile of wall .. 1

EXAMPLE 13: Partially melded hand. Last tile of wall was 3 character. East round; dealer.

$(20 + 4 + 0 + 2 + 0 + 0 + 2) \times 2 = 56$
Each player pays 2×60 to dealer

20 for winning; 4 for concealed triplet of simples; 0 for sequence; 2 for melded triplet of simples; 0 for sequence; 0 for pair; 2 for self-drawn tile. One double for last tile of wall.

Last Discarded Tile: If you go out with the very last discarded tile, after the last tile from the wall has been drawn, you receive one double. You are paid by the player who discarded the tile, as usual.

Going out with last discarded tile   **1**

EXAMPLE 14: Partially melded hand. Last tile discarded, by West, was 2 bamboo. East round; dealer.

$$(20 + 2 + 4 + 4 + 0 + 0) \times 2 = 60$$

West pays 6 × 60 to dealer

20 for winning; 2 for melded triplet of simples; 4 for melded triplet of honors; 4 for melded triplet of honors; 0 for sequence; 0 for pair. One double for last discarded tile.

Robbing a Kong: If another player draws a tile and adds it to a melded triplet to make a melded four, you may go out using that tile, breaking up his four. For this you receive one double. You are paid by the maker of the four, just as if he had discarded the tile.

Going out by robbing a kong...   **1**

EXAMPLE 15: Partially melded hand. Tile robbed from four (of North) was 1 dot. West round; dealer.

$$(20 + 0 + 0 + 4 + 0 + 0) \times 2 = 48$$

North pays 6 × 50 to dealer

20 for winning; 0 for sequence; 0 for sequence; 4 for melded triplet of honors; 0 for sequence; 0 for pair. One double for robbing a kong.

Supplement Tile: If you have just made a four, concealed or melded, and then can go out with the supplement tile drawn for the four, you receive one double. This is treated as going out self-drawn, for which you are given two points, and the set you complete with the supplement tile is considered to be concealed.

Going out with a supplement tile..   **1**

EXAMPLE 16: Partially melded hand. Supplement tile was 6 character. East round; player is South.

C   M

$$(20 + 4 + 8 + 0 + 0 + 0 + 2) \times 2 = 68$$
Non-dealers pay 70; dealer pays 140

20 for winning; 4 for concealed triplet of simples; 8 for melded four of simples; 0 for each sequence and for pair; 2 for self-drawn tile. One double for going out with a supplement tile.

Doubles for Special Inclusions

In the popular game, certain groups of sequences and one group of triplets, as explained on page 81, can earn doubles. Officially, only three consecutive sequences are given any credit.

Three Consecutive Sequences: Three consecutive sequences in one suit (that is, a continuous run from one to nine) are worth one double.
1 through 9 of one suit   1

EXAMPLE 17: Concealed hand. Discarded tile, by East, was 2 character. East round; player is West.

C

$$(20 + 0 + 0 + 0 + 4 + 2 + 2 + 10) \times 2 = 76$$
Dealer pays 4 × 80 to West

20 for winning; 0 for each sequence; 4 for concealed triplet of simples; 2 for lucky pair; 2 for one-chance; 10 for concealed hand with discarded tile. One double for three consecutive sequences.

Double for No-Points

A peculiar situation arises occasionally in Mah Jong when a hand has no point value other than the 20 points for winning. Its "0" total earns it a double for its very consistency. The feeling is that the low score otherwise received does not reflect the difficulty of achieving such a hand.

If this zero-hand happens to be a concealed hand completed with a discarded tile, the 10 points for this are added to the 20 points for winning, making 30, and then this total is multiplied by 2 for the double.

The fact that it may have no *points* does not exclude the possibility that it may have other *doubles*, for example for the run from 1 to 9 mentioned above, or for "all simples."

A no-points hand has the following characteristics:

   a) It has four sequences.
   b) The pair does not consist of lucky tiles.
   c) It went out with a discarded tile.
   d) It was not a one-chance hand.

No-points hands can qualify for the following doubles:

   a) Going out with last tile of wall.
   b) Going out with last discarded tile.
   c) Going out with a supplement tile.
   d) Going out by robbing a kong.
   e) Three consecutive sequences.
   f) All simples.
   g) Terminal or honor in each set, but only with four sequences and a pair of ordinary winds.
   h) One suit with honors, but only with four sequences and a pair of ordinary winds.
   i) One suit only.
   j) Concealed self-drawn hand, but only if "Self-drawn eighty," explained on page 52, is permitted.

EXAMPLE 18: Concealed hand. Discarded tile, by East, was 9 bamboo. South round; player is North.

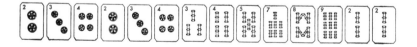

$$(20 + 0 + 0 + 0 + 0 + 0 + 10) \times 2 = 60$$

East pays 4 × 60 to North

20 for winning; 0 for every set; 10 for concealed hand with discarded tile. One double for no-points.

EXAMPLE 19: Partially melded hand. Discarded tile, by East, was 3 character. South round; player is North.

$$(20 + 0 + 0 + 0 + 0 + 0) \times 2 = 40$$
East pays 4 × 40 to North

20 for winning; 0 for each set. One double for no-points.

EXAMPLE 20: Partially melded hand. Discarded tile, by East, was 4 character. South round; player is North.

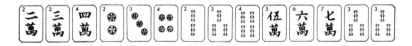

$$(20 + 0 + 0 + 0 + 0 + 0) \times 4 = 80$$
East pays 4 × 80 to North

20 for winning; 0 for each set. One double for all simples; one double for no-points.

Self-Drawn Eighty (Optional): A concealed no-point hand that happened to go out self-drawn would earn 20 points for winning, plus 2 for self drawn, totaling 22 points, and thus the hand would no longer qualify as a no-points hand. Players often agree beforehand to allow the player who finds himself in this situation to forgo the 2 points and claim his double for a no-points hand, as well as the double for concealed self-drawn. In this case the 2 points are simply not added in the total. If such agreement is not made before the game, this optional rule is not in force.

To avoid confusion it should be restated here that a true no-points hand can only be one that totals 20 for winning or 30 for winning plus having a concealed hand that goes out on a discard. Any other total, even if it is between 20 and 30 does not qualify as a no-points hand, hence the above option.

In any case, the above optional rule applies only to a *concealed* no-points hand. Players should not confuse this with a partially-melded hand which goes out self drawn.

EXAMPLE 21: Concealed hand. Self-drawn tile was 1 bamboo. South round; player is South.

Scoring without self-drawn eighty: $(20 + 0 + 0 + 0 + 0 + 0 + 2) \times 2 = 44$
Non-dealers pay 40; dealer pays 80
20 for winning; 0 for each set; 2 for self-drawn tile. One double for concealed self-drawn hand.

Scoring with self-drawn eighty: $(20 + 0 + 0 + 0 + 0 + 0 + 0) \times 4 = 80$
Non-dealers pay 80; dealer pays 160
20 for winning; 0 for each set; 2 for self-drawn tile is not credited. One double for concealed self-drawn hand; one double for no-points.

Doubles for Consistency

There are three points of view from which the calculation of doubles for consistency can be figured. When scoring, the player should first apply one, then, after exhausting all its possibilities, proceed to the next system of figuring. He can thus simplify the approach to this rather complicated system.

The first of these points of view groups the tiles according to the difficulty with which they are collected and combined. By this system, the honors fall into the "most difficult" group, because they can only be combined into triplets. The terminals are the "next-most-difficult" because they can be combined into triplets and restricted types of sequences. The simples are the "easiest" because they can make many kinds of sequences and triplets.

All Simples: A hand that contains no honors or terminals is fairly easy to make, but is given one double because of its consistency.

All simples **1**

EXAMPLE 22: Partially melded hand. Discarded tile, by West, was 3 dot. West round; player is East.

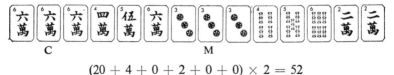

C   M

$(20 + 4 + 0 + 2 + 0 + 0) \times 2 = 52$
West pays 6×50 to dealer
20 for winning; 4 for concealed triplet of simples; 0 for sequence; 2 for melded triplet of simples; 0 for sequence; 0 for pair. One double for all simples.

All Terminals and Honors: The opposite extreme is the hand that contains nothing but terminals and honors. This hand is necessarily a four-triplets hand, and almost invariably receives extra doubles for lucky sets. By virtue of containing no simples, it receives one double. The point count is usually very high, and often the score reaches the limit.

All terminals and honors **1**

EXAMPLE 23: Partially melded hand. Self-drawn tile was 1 dot. East round; player is West.

M   C   M   C

$(20 + 4 + 8 + 4 + 8 + 2 + 2) \times 4 = 192$

Non-dealers pay 190; dealer pays 380

20 for winning; 4 for melded triplet of honors; 8 for concealed triplet of terminals; 4 for melded triplet of terminals; 8 for concealed triplet of terminals; 2 for lucky pair; 2 for self-drawn tile. One double for all terminals and honors; one double for four triplets.

Terminal or Honor in Each Set: A less extreme case is that in which every set is composed, at least partially, of terminals or honors. It may take two forms: either it includes a terminal in every set, or it includes some honor sets and a terminal in every remaining set. In either case it receives one double, and is likely to score high, because it often receives extra doubles for lucky sets.

Terminal or honor in each set. .   **1**

EXAMPLE 24: Partially melded hand. Discarded tile, by West, was 3 character. East round; player is South.

M

$(20 + 0 + 0 + 0 + 4 + 2 + 2) \times 4 = 112$

West pays 4×110 to South

20 for winning; 0 for each sequence; 4 for melded triplet of honors; 2 for lucky pair; 2 for one-chance. One double for lucky set of green dragons; one double for terminal or honor in each set.

EXAMPLE 25: Partially melded hand. Discarded tile, by West, was 2 dot. East round; player is South.

C

$$(20 + 8 + 0 + 0 + 0 + 0 + 2) \times 2 = 60$$
West pays 4 × 60 to South

20 for winning; 8 for concealed triplet of terminals; 0 for each sequence; 0 for the pair; 2 for one-chance. One double for terminal or honor in each set.

Another classification of the tiles in the calculation of doubles for consistency divides them into the individual suits. A hand which contains only one suit is a high-scoring hand.

One suit with honors: A hand that has some sets of honors, but whose other tiles are all of one suit receives one double.

One suit with honors **1**

EXAMPLE 26: Partially melded hand. Discarded tile, by West, was red dragon. West round; player is North.

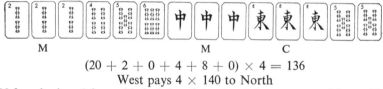

M   M   C

$$(20 + 2 + 0 + 4 + 8 + 0) \times 4 = 136$$
West pays 4 × 140 to North

20 for winning; 2 for melded triplet of simples; 0 for sequence; 4 for melded triplet of honors; 8 for concealed triplet of honors; 0 for pair. One double for one suit with honors; one double for lucky set of red dragons.

One Suit Only: A hand that is composed of the tiles of one suit alone, without honors, receives four doubles.

One suit only **4**

EXAMPLE 27: Partially melded hand. Self-drawn tile was 5 character. East round; player is East.

M

$$(20 + 0 + 0 + 0 + 8 + 0 + 2) \times 16 = 480$$
Each player pays 2 × 480 to dealer

20 for winning; 0 for each sequence; 8 for melded four of simples; 0 for pair; 2 for self-drawn tile. Four doubles for one suit only.

Finally, in calculating doubles for consistency, the honors can be considered separately as dragons and winds. A hand containing one set of each of the dragons, or one set of each of the winds, is a very high-scoring hand, regardless of what the other sets may be.

Little Three Dragons: A hand with two triplets and a pair of dragons receives one double in addition to the two doubles from the lucky sets.
                    Dragons: 2 triplets and a pair..   1

EXAMPLE 28: Partially melded hand. Discarded tile, by East, was 2 character. East round; player is North.

$$(20 + 4 + 4 + 0 + 0 + 2) \times 8 = 240$$
East pays 4 × 240 to North

20 for winning; 4 for each melded triplet of honors; 0 for each sequence; 2 for lucky pair. One double for Little Three Dragons; one double for each lucky set—red and green dragons.

Big Three Dragons, and the Four-Winds hands are limit hands described below.

THE LIMIT

After totaling the winner's points and multiplying them by any doubles, the next thing is for the other players to pay him. His total score may be anywhere from 22 points to whatever limit has been decided upon—officially 500 points. Losers then pay the winner according to the rules under "Paying the Winner" on page 59. This will be based upon his final score, which is his total score rounded out to the nearest 10.

The limit can be achieved in two ways: first, if the score itself exceeds the limit; and secondly, if the hand qualifies automatically in any of the ways listed below.

It is convenient to remember that with a limit of 500, any hand that has five doubles exceeds the maximum score (32 (for five doubles) × 20 (minimum score possible) = 640). The same is true of any hand with four doubles and 32 or more points (16 (for four doubles) × 32 = 512).

The ten hands listed below are automatic limit hands.

Big Three Dragons: A hand containing one triplet of each of the dragons is a limit hand. The other sets may be any sets that complete the hand.

Dragons: 3 triplets

Little Four Winds: A hand containing one triplet of each of three winds and a pair of the fourth is a limit hand. The other set may be any set that completes the hand.

Winds: 3 triplets and pair

Big Four Winds: A hand containing one triplet of each of the four winds is a limit hand. The pair may be any two matching tiles.

Winds: 4 triplets

All Honors: Any hand containing *only wind and dragon tiles* is a limit hand. It must consist of four triplets and a pair.

Honors: 4 triplets and pair

All Terminals: Any hand containing only terminal tiles ·is a limit hand. It must consist of four triplets and a pair.

Terminals: 4 triplets and pair

Four Concealed Triplets: A hand containing four concealed triplets of any kind is a limit hand. The four triplets must be made completely with tiles drawn from the wall. The pair alone may include a discarded tile. Thus if you have almost completed a hand of four concealed triplets, and are waiting with two pairs, you must draw the third member to either pair from the wall. If you already have four complete triplets and are waiting with an isolated tile to make the pair, you may claim someone's discarded tile.

Four concealed triplets

Heavenly Hand: If the dealer goes out immediately with the hand he is dealt, he receives the limit. (Recall that the dealer draws fourteen tiles at the beginning of the game.) It makes no difference what the hand consists of, so long as it is complete, with four sets of three and a pair. He is paid by all three players, as if he went out self-drawn.

Dealer goes out on dealt hand

Earthly Hand: If a non-dealer goes out on the *first discard made by the dealer,* or if he goes out *self-drawn in his first turn* before "chow," "pung" or "kong" is declared, he receives the limit. In the first case, the dealer must pay him; in the second he is paid by all three losers.

A hand is given no special credit if it goes out on any discard other than the dealer's, even at the very beginning of the game.

Non-dealer goes out
On dealer's first discard, or
Self-drawn in first turn

Nine Gates: This hand is composed entirely of one suit, and contains a triplet of ones, a run from two to eight, and a triplet of nines. The fourteenth tile may match any of these. Inspection will show that any such hand is actually a complete hand containing four sets of three and a pair. The player must make a ready hand which includes the two triplets and the run from two to eight, and must go out by claiming, or drawing the odd tile.

The hand must be a true nine-chance hand having nine openings, or "gates." That is, it must be completely concealed, and such that the player can actually go out on any tile of that suit.

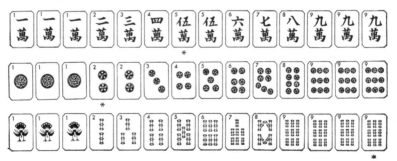

* Last tile

**One suit only: triplet of ones, triplet
of nines, run from 2 to 8, and any odd
tile drawn last**

Thirteen Orphans: This hand is composed entirely of terminals and honors, and contains one lone tile of each. Thus: three different dragons, four different winds, three different ones and three different nines. The fourteenth tile may match any of these. The hand must of course be concealed, but the player may make a ready hand which already includes the odd tile, and go out by claiming or drawing the last honor or terminal he needs.

Terminals and honors: one of each, with one to match

PAYING THE WINNER

The system of paying the winner has recently been revised by the Japan Mah Jong Association. The old system, which was also used in America in the nineteen thirties, is described on page 90. The modern system of payment, now official in Japan, seems to be the fairest of all so far devised, and adds interest to the game, making defensive play as important as offensive.

Players should always be aware of the intentions of their opponents, even if no melds are showing. It should be clear from a player's discards alone what kind of hand he is constructing, and discards that serve his purposes should always be avoided. Thus, the person who discards any tile that enables another player to go out pays for all three losers.

Two principles apply in paying. First, the dealer must always pay or be paid double. Second, if one player must pay the whole loss, he pays the total amount the winner would have received from all three losers, including double for the dealer. This works out as follows:

Dealer Goes Out Self-Drawn: Each non-dealer pays double score.
Dealer Goes Out on a Discard: Discarder pays 6 × score.
Non-Dealer Goes Out Self-Drawn: Dealer pays double; each non-dealer pays single score.
Non-Dealer Goes Out on a Discard: Discarder pays 4 × score.

Penalty Payment: If any penalty lower than one-half the limit is exacted during the hand, the fine is placed in the center of the table. The winner collects this fine at the end of the hand. If the hand is a draw, or if the offender himself wins the hand, he reclaims the fine.

Rounding Off: The Japanese differ on the matter of rounding off the score, but most agree on a method similar to that given here. For other methods used in Japan, see page 90. The system below is the one officially endorsed.

1. Calculate the points and add 20 for winning.
2. Multiply by two for each double.
3. Round off to the nearest 10 (04 is 00; 06 is 10).
4. The number obtained is the *final score*, which is then multiplied for payment.

Whatever method is used, it should be used consistently, as a minor change can have a major effect on the score.

The scoring outline at the beginning of this chapter may be useful for beginners.

Alternatives, Variations and Additions

Here in *Part Two* are included all of the alternatives, additions and variations on Mah Jong that are likely to be of interest to American players of the game. Many of them may also be useful to those who play in China or Japan with groups that abide by their own private rules.

If readers who are familiar with the Chinese game find that there are any additions that would be appropriate to this chapter, I would be interested in hearing from them, in care of the publisher.

The first four chapters below correspond respectively, in subject matter, to those in *Part One. Chapter Five*, in turn, summarizes the American scoring rules of the 1920's.

The Mah Jong Set

TILES

Flower and Season Tiles

These are no longer used in Mah Jong, but still appear in some sets. For those who wish to play with them, the rules for their use are given below.

Description: There are sometimes four and sometimes eight of these tiles. The patterns vary immensely, but each of the four flowers and each of the four seasons is assigned to a wind, as below:

Winds:	East	South	West	North
Flowers:	Plum	Orchid	Chrysanthemum	Bamboo
Seasons:	Spring	Summer	Autumn	Winter

Thus each player has an "own wind," an "own flower" and an "own season." For example, West's own wind is West; his own flower is the chrysanthemum, and his own season is autumn.

Building the Wall: When all eight flowers and seasons are used, they are mixed with the other tiles, and each player builds a row of eighteen, instead of seventeen, stacks. If only four are used, East and West build eighteen-stack rows and North and South build seventeen-stack rows.

Dealt Hand: When the hands are dealt, and before play begins, each player melds (places face up on his right) all flowers and seasons, and draws supplement tiles from the dead wall to replace them. East moves first, followed by South, West and North, and then the drawing and discarding begin.

During Play: If a player draws a flower or season during play, he melds it and draws a supplement tile to replace it.

Scoring: The flowers and seasons are scored as explained on page 79.

ACCESSORIES

Discs

Occasionally the set includes four discs made of bone, each of which bears one of the characters for a wind: East, South, West and North. If these are present in the set, they are used instead of four wind tiles to determine the seating arrangement for the game. They are placed upside-down on the table, mixed, arranged in a row, and treated as described on page 21.

The Jongg

If the set includes discs, the round box in which they come can be used instead of the dice to indicate who is dealing. The dealer keeps it in front of him as a means of identification. In the American game of the 1920's, "passing the deal" was sometimes called "passing the jongg." The name seems to have originated in America and has nothing to do with the name of the game.

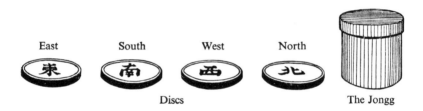

East   South   West   North

Discs   The Jongg

CHAPTER TWO

Preliminaries

BEFORE THE GAME

Seating Arrangement and Selecting the First Dealer (American and Japanese)

The official system of determining the seating arrangement for the game is complex, and involves four throws of the dice. Some Japanese and many Americans prefer to substitute this simpler method: Mix four wind tiles, one of each wind, face down on the table. Let each player draw one. The player who draws East is *dealer* and has the choice of seats. South sits on his right, West opposite him, and North on his left.

The only important thing in placing the players is that they should be seated at random.

BEFORE EACH HAND

Breaking the Wall

Occasionally the location of the break in the wall is determined by one throw of the dice instead of two. In this case, the number that appears on the dice indicates both the player whose row of tiles will be broken, and the number of stacks to be separated from the right end of the row.

EXAMPLE

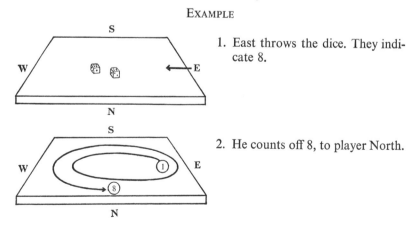

1. East throws the dice. They indicate 8.

2. He counts off 8, to player North.

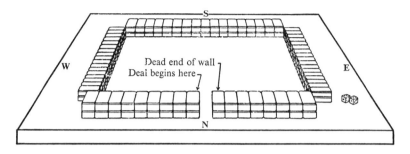

3. He breaks the wall after the 8th stack in North's row. The deal begins with the 9th stack.

Loose Tiles

It used to be the custom to establish a pair of loose tiles on top of the dead wall. These were used as supplement tiles. The procedure was as follows: After determining the location of the break in the wall, the stack immediately to the right of the break is lifted from the wall. The two tiles are dropped face down on top of the wall to the right of the break. The lower tile is placed next to the break, and the upper tile to its right. These two tiles are used to supplement fours; the one furthest from the break is drawn first. Whenever both of them are drawn, another stack from the right of the break is set on the wall. The loose tiles are maintained by the player in front of whom they are located.

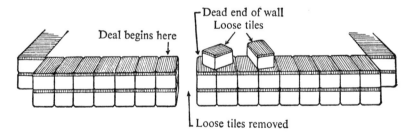

The Deal (American)

In the American game, "chan-chan" is sometimes omitted from the deal. After each player has drawn twelve tiles, the dealer takes only one. South, West and North draw one each in turn, and finally the dealer draws another tile to make a hand of fourteen.

CHAPTER THREE
Playing

CHOW, PUNG AND KONG (JAPANESE)

Occasionally, to speed up the game, Japanese players allow the following order of moves in claiming a tile:

Chow and Pung

1. Declare.
2. Discard a tile first, allowing the next player to go ahead.
3. Meld the set.
4. Add the claimed tile to the set.

Kong

1. Declare.
2. Draw a supplement tile.
3. Discard a tile.
4. Meld the triplet.
5. Add the claimed tile to the triplet.

ARRANGEMENT OF TILES

During the Game: Tiles in the hand are arranged in any order. Melded sets are placed face up on the player's right, in any order, while a concealed four is distinguished from a melded four by turning the two outside tiles face down:

Melded sequence   Melded triplet   Melded four   Concealed four

On Winning: For convenience in scoring, the Japanese use the following system of displaying the winning hand. The purposes are: first, to distinguish a one-chance hand (2 points); second, to distinguish a self-drawn tile (2 points); third, to differentiate between a melded and concealed triplet; and fourth, to distinguish between a melded and concealed four.

One-chance is indicated by standing the tile on end in its set, and self-drawn is indicated by placing the tile flat on top of its set:

End of terminal sequence   Middle of sequence   Pair   Self-drawn

Thus one-chance *and* self-drawn are indicated by standing the tile on end on top of its set:

   End of terminal sequence   Middle of sequence   Pair

One-chance and self-drawn

A concealed triplet is identified by placing one of its three members on top of the other two, and if a self-drawn tile completes a concealed triplet, it is placed on end on top of the other two:

Concealed triplet   Concealed triplet self-drawn

Other sets are simply placed flat, including a triplet that was completed by a discarded tile:

Other melded or concealed sets

DRAW (JAPANESE)

Draw Rules

The official rules as revised in 1956 state that a draw is declared only in the event that no one goes out before the wall, excepting fourteen tiles, is exhausted. The complete rules, previous to the revision, included five cases in which a draw could be declared, and these are still widely used.

When No One Has Gone Out: As described in *Part One, page 32.*

Nine Different Terminals and Honors: If a player has been dealt nine or more of the thirteen different terminals and honors (including his first draw), he may declare a drawn hand. The declaration may only be made before anyone has said "chow," "pung" or "kong," and within the first round of discards: either before the dealer's first discard, or in the player's own turn.

On the other hand, this player may try to make a limit hand of one of each of the thirteen tiles.

Four Fours: When four sets of fours are made, either melded or concealed, a draw is declared. The fourth four-maker may not draw a supplement tile. But if anyone can go out by "robbing the kong," this is permitted.

If four fours is permitted as a limit hand, then an exception to this rule is made if one player makes all four fours. In this case the game continues, and if he goes out he receives the limit. However, a fifth four brings the game to an end in any case.

Identical First Four Discards: If, in the first round of discards, every player discards the same tile, a draw is declared.

Three Declare "Out"; If a tile is discarded and three people declare "out," no one may go out. A draw is declared. If two people declare "out," the one who would have played first gets the tile.

Payment in a Draw

Some Japanese players have added the rule that points should be exchanged after a draw, if any player's hand is ready to go out. 600 points are paid in all as described below:

If Three Players' Hands are Ready: The one whose hand is not ready pays 200 points to each.

If Two Players' Hands are Ready: The two whose hands are not ready each pay 300 points.

If One Player's Hand is Ready: The other three each pay him 200 points.

Of course, if all four players' hands are ready, or if none are, no points are exchanged.

After a Draw

The official rules state that the deal should always pass after a draw. Some players prefer to allow the dealer to deal again. Others permit the dealer to deal again if his hand was ready, and have the deal pass if it was not. If one of these alternatives is selected, the retained deal should be called a *redeal* to distinguish it from a *dealer's extra hand*, due to the bonus often used for the latter, as described on page 89.

DEALER'S EXTRA HAND (JAPANESE)

If East wins, he retains the deal, and the hand played is in all ways similar to an ordinary hand, according to the Japan Mah Jong Association Rules. The bonus, which is a popular addition to the dealer's extra hand rule, necessitates that East should place a 10-point bone on the table to signify that he is playing an extra hand. The winner of this hand collects, in addition to his score, 100 points from each loser, or 300 points from the discarder if the winner goes out on a discarded tile.

If East wins, he collects the bonus, which is not doubled for the dealer, and adds a second 10-point bone to the first. This signifies that he is playing a second extra hand, and the winner will collect 200 points from each loser as a bonus, or 600 points from the discarder. For a third extra hand, East places a third 10-point bone on the table and the winner collects 900 points. This may continue until East loses, at which time the deal passes, or until he wins an eighth extra hand. For this he receives the limit, and the deal passes.

It is wise not to use this rule unless many other additions to the game are also made, and the limit is raised to 1500 points.

READY

The rule of "riichi" is very popular in Japan, though it complicates the game, as explained in the introduction to this book on page 12. Due to its increasingly widespread use, the Japan Mah Jong Association has defined a new game, called "Riichi Mah Jong," in which this rule is included, and the scoring values are adjusted to a higher level. Only a brief description of "ready" is given here. If players wish to use it. I suggest that the limit be adjusted to 1500, and that all the special inclusions mentioned below under "Scoring" be added to the rules.

Ready Hand

When your hand requires only one tile to make it complete, it is called ready. It may be that only one particular tile will complete it (for example, when you have four complete sets and an isolated tile which you are waiting to match for the pair), or it may be that one of several tiles will do (a sequence of 3-4-5-6-7, for example, can be completed with a 2 to make 2-3-4 and 5-6-7, or with a 5 to make 3-4-5 and 5-6-7, or with an 8 to make 3-4-5 and 6-7-8).

Declaring "Ready" (Japanese)

When your hand is ready you may declare "ready." You must then place your hand face down on the table and place a 100-point bone on it. It is also the convention, when declaring "ready," to place your discard at right angles to the others, so that your opponents will know what discards were previous, and what subsequent, to your declaration.

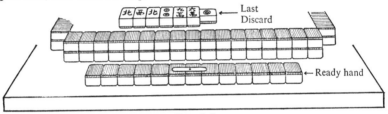

"Ready"

The following rules apply to the "ready" declaration.

Concealed Hand: The hand must be completely concealed. It may include a concealed four.

Changes: No changes may be made in the hand after the declaration. A concealed four may not be made after the declaration.

Drawing: After the declaration, you must draw from the wall without looking at your hand. Simply turn over a tile from the wall when it is your turn, and if you cannot use it to go out, discard it.

Retraction: The declaration cannot be retracted.

Going Out: The declaration commits you to going out with *any* tile that will complete your hand. For example, if you are waiting to complete a 7-8 serial pair, and a 6 is discarded, you must go out, even if you would have preferred a 9.

Scoring: A hand that goes out after declaring "ready" receives one double.

Forfeit: If another player goes out, you must forfeit the 100 points to him.

Etiquette: After declaring "ready" and placing his hand face-down on the table, a player should not look at the hands of his opponents.

Delayed Call (American)

Here is a "ready" rule that is often included in the American game. It states that a player may declare "ready" if his hand is ready in the very first turn, and that subsequently on going out he will receive one double. The American system calls for the following conditions:

1. Only a non-dealer in the first round of discards may declare.
2. The hand must be placed face-down and no changes may subsequently be made.
3. Draws from the wall should be turned over and discarded if they cannot be used to go out.
4. The declaration may not be retracted.
5. A hand that goes out after declaring "ready" receives one double.
6. A player is not obligated to go out on any tile that completes his hand, and no forfeit is made if another player wins.

SACRED DISCARD (JAPANESE)

The official rules state that you may go out on a tile identical to one you yourself have discarded, provided only that you have drawn at least once from the wall subsequent to making the discard. Popularly, however, some other rules are in force.

Sacred Discard Rule

Sometimes players agree not to allow a player to use a sacred discard at all. Then if you have discarded a tile which you subsequently need to complete a set, you must obtain the duplicate only by drawing it from the wall. In this case, you can go out self-drawn, or by claiming any discarded tile which will complete your hand other than the one identical to your discard.

If only this one sacred discard rule is in force, and you have a sacred discard, you may not declare "ready."

1-4-7 Rule

If the above sacred discard rule is adopted, the 1-4-7 rule may be added to it. This restricts the player still further. It applies to the special case in which a hand is ready with a serial pair, and a sacred discard is showing which would complete the sequence at one end. The rule forbids a player to go out by completing either end of the sequence, except by drawing the necessary tile from the wall. In this case, you can go out self-drawn, or by claiming any discarded tile which will complete a set other than the set which could be completed by your sacred discard.

The 1-4-7 rule is explained in full, with examples, immediately after the next paragraph.

"Sacred Discard" Declaration

If one or both of the two optional rules above are in force, they may be modified by allowing a player to declare "sacred discard." Having made the declaration, a player may then go out on any tile that will complete his hand. The declaration does not tell his opponents which is the sacred tile, but it warns them to be careful in discarding. He is then justified in going out if another player discards the sacred tile.

If this declaration is allowed, a player may declare "ready" and "sacred discard" simultaneously.

Explanation of the 1-4-7 Rule

Experts often agree to use this rule because it is quite useful for good defensive play. In order to discard wisely one must be able to depend upon the evidence of one's opponents' discards. On the other hand, if it is not used, one has the opportunity to bluff, by intentionally making a ready hand waiting for a tile identical or related to one's own discards.

The rule applies to the special case when your hand is ready with a sequence which could be completed in more than one way, and you have a sacred discard. It forbids you to use a tile discarded by another player to complete any set which your sacred discard could complete.

The following examples will illustrate the difference between the simple sacred discard rule and the sacred discard rule as used with the 1-4-7 rule.

EXAMPLE 1: Ready with isolated tile and sacred discard.

Sacred discard   Your hand   Waiting for 1 dot

The two rules have the same effect in this case: if another player discards the same tile, you may not go out. You may only go out by drawing the tile.

EXAMPLE 2: Ready with one-chance sequence and sacred discard.

Sacred discard   Your hand   Waiting for 7 character

The two rules have the same effect in this case: if another player discards the same tile, you may not go out. You may only go out by drawing the tile.

EXAMPLE 3: Ready with two pairs and sacred discard.

Sacred discard   Your hand   Waiting for 2 or 5 dot

The two rules have the same effect in this case: if another player discards the 2, you may not go out. If another player discards the 5, you may go out. You may also go out by drawing either the 2 or the 5.

EXAMPLE 4: Ready with serial pair and sacred discard.

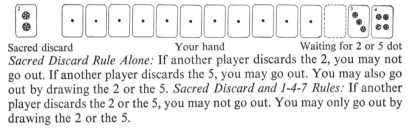

Sacred discard   Your hand   Waiting for 2 or 5 dot

Sacred Discard Rule Alone: If another player discards the 2, you may not go out. If another player discards the 5, you may go out. You may also go out by drawing the 2 or the 5. *Sacred Discard and 1-4-7 Rules:* If another player discards the 2 or the 5, you may not go out. You may only go out by drawing the 2 or the 5.

EXAMPLE 5: Ready with run of five and a terminal sacred discard.

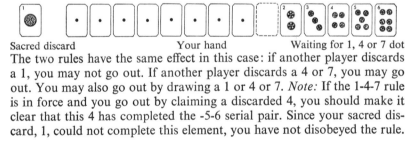

Sacred discard   Your hand   Waiting for 1, 4 or 7 dot

The two rules have the same effect in this case: if another player discards a 1, you may not go out. If another player discards a 4 or 7, you may go out. You may also go out by drawing a 1 or 4 or 7. *Note:* If the 1-4-7 rule is in force and you go out by claiming a discarded 4, you should make it clear that this 4 has completed the -5-6 serial pair. Since your sacred discard, 1, could not complete this element, you have not disobeyed the rule.

EXAMPLE 6: Ready with run of five and middle-of-run sacred discard.

Sacred discard   Your hand   Waiting for 1, 4 or 7 dot

Sacred Discard Rule Alone: If another player discards a 4, you may not go out. If another player discards a 1 or 7, you may go out. You may also go out by drawing a 1 or 4 or 7. *Sacred Discard and 1-4-7 Rules:* If another player discards a 1 or 4 or 7, you may not go out. You may go out only by drawing the 1 or 4 or 7 from the wall. The reason is that your sacred discard, 4, could complete either the 2-3- or the -5-6 serial pair, hence using a 1 or 7 to complete either of these is against the rule.

INSURANCE PENALTIES

The following are cases that rarely arise, but which are sometimes pro-vided-for in order to insure that others shall not be unfairly penalized if one player makes an irresponsible move. Usually, when a player goes out on a discard, the discarder of the winning tile is held responsible. When a player goes out self-drawn, no one of his opponents is held to be more guilty than the others.

Occasionally, however, a discard made *any time during the game* may enable a player finally to make a limit hand. In this case, the discarder of the tile that made the limit hand possible is held responsible and must pay all losses. Following are the four situations involved.

1. Player A has melded two triplets (or fours) of dragons. Player B dis-cards the third dragon. Player A claims it and melds a third dragon-triplet. If A subsequently goes out *either self-drawn or on any discard*, B must pay all losses.

2. Player A has melded three triplets (or fours) of winds. Player B dis-cards the fourth wind. Player A claims it and melds a fourth wind-triplet. If A subsequently goes out *either self-drawn or on any discard*, B must pay all losses.

3. Player A has melded three triplets (or fours) of honors. Player B dis-cards another honor. Player A claims it and melds a fourth honor-triplet. If A subsequently goes out *self-drawn on an honor tile*, B must pay all losses·

4. Player A has melded three triplets (or fours) of terminals. Player B discards another terminal. Player A claims it and melds a fourth terminal-triplet. If A subsequently goes out *self-drawn on a terminal tile*, B must pay all losses.

If "all green" has been selected by the players as a limit hand, a similar rule should be in force about "green" tiles.

THREE- AND FIVE-HANDED GAMES

Mah Jong is an excellent game for four people. It is not as well-suited, however, to three or five, but it is perfectly possible, as described below.

Three-Handed Game

Order of Play: There are three hands to a round, and four rounds to a game. In the first hand, omit the West wind tiles from the set. Players are East, South and North. In the second hand, omit the South wind tiles; players are East, West and North. In the third hand, omit the North tiles;

players are East, South and West. The deal rotates as in the ordinary game. In the illustration below, numbers indicate players.

One round of three hands

The Deal: Each player builds a *sixteen*-stack row in front of him, instead of seventeen as in the regular game (or seventeen instead of eighteen, if the flowers and seasons are used). Each then draws a hand of twelve tiles at random from the thirty-six tiles remaining on the table. East then throws the dice to determine where the wall shall be broken, counting the actual players counterclockwise, beginning with himself. The player selected breaks the wall and East takes two tiles from the left of the break to make a hand of fourteen. The others take one each in order, and East begins by discarding.

Play is the same as in the regular game.

Winning Hands: It is impossible to make the following hands, due to the omission of one set of wind tiles:

> Little Four Winds
> Big Four Winds
> Heavenly Twins (seven pairs, all honors)
> Thirteen Orphans

Five-Handed Game

One suit tile is shufflled with the four wind tiles before drawing for seats. The player who draws the suit tile sits out through the first hand of play. At the end of the hand, East steps out, and the player sitting out becomes North in the next hand. In the illustration below, numbers indicate players.

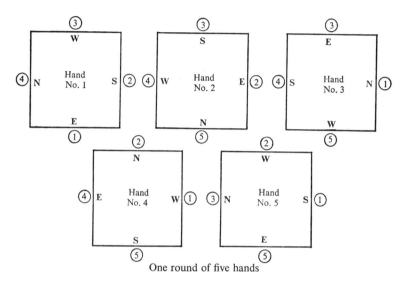

One round of five hands

Thus there are five hands to a round, each player playing four of them. Play is in all other respects the same as in the regular game.

CHAPTER FOUR

Scoring

INITIAL POINTS AND THE LIMIT

The official rules provide that the limit should be set at 500, and each of the players should receive 2000 points' worth of bones at the start of the game. Popularly, however, many players prefer to distribute more bones initially, and some like to raise the limit. Two alternative distributions of bones per player are given below:

Value	Number	Total	Limit
10	10	100	
100	9	900	
1000	2	2000	
		3000	500
10	10	100	
100	9	900	
1000	2	2000	
5000	1	5000	
		8000	1000 or 1500

The latter distribution is often the simplest when a high scoring system is used, as it saves the trouble of keeping track of debts, should that become necessary.

POINTS

Points for Winning (Chinese)

In the Chinese game it is often provided that a player should receive 10 instead of 20 points for winning.

For winning **10**

Points for Sets

All variations of Mah Jong are similar in respect to points given for sets.

Points for Flowers and Seasons

When flower or season tiles are used, 4 points are awarded for each such tile held. See page 63 and the explanation under "Doubles" below for additional information on flowers and seasons.

Flower or season .... 4 points each

Points for Last Tile of Hand (American)

In the American game, both the 2 points for a self-drawn tile and the 2 points for a one-chance hand may always be discounted if a player chooses, thus making possible a "no-points" hand that would otherwise not be allowed. The only requirement for this hand is that the sets themselves should not score, thus its American name is "all sequences."

All games are similar in that self-drawn and one-chance are each worth 2 points, except as noted above.

Points for Concealed Hand (American and Chinese)

In China and America, no credit is given for a concealed hand.

Concealed hand
With discarded tile .... no credit
Self-drawn ... 2 (no extra credit)

DOUBLES

The following is a complete list of all the winning hands qualifying for doubles under any system. Players may wish to select some or all of them. Those who are familiar with a particular variety of Mah Jong will find here, if not in *Part One* of this book, all the hands they are accustomed to score.

Doubles for Lucky Sets (Flowers and Seasons)

All games are similar with respect to sets of lucky tiles. However, when flower and season tiles are used (see page 63), additional doubles are obtained from them:

Flower or season .... 4 points each
Own flower .... 1 double
Own season .... 1 double
"Bouquet" of four flowers. 4 doubles
"Bouquet" of four seasons. 4 doubles

There is no flower or season to correspond to the "prevailing wind"; only the "own" flower and season are special. If both are held, the player receives two doubles. The four doubles for a bouquet include the double for the "own" flower or season within it. Thus the highest number of doubles a player can receive from these tiles is five: four for a bouquet (of four flowers, for example), and one extra (for his own season).

Flower and season tiles do not count as part of the hand. Therefore it is perfectly permissible to have "one suit only" or "all simples," etc., with flowers or seasons or both.

EXAMPLE 1: Partially melded hand. Discarded tile, by West, was 1 character. East round; player is North.

$$(20 + 4 + 0 + 2 + 0 + 0 + 2 + 4 + 4 + 4) \times 8 = 320$$

West pays 4 × 320 to North

20 for winning; 4 for melded triplet of honors; 0 for sequence; 2 for melded triplet of simples; 0 for sequence; 0 for pair; 2 for one-chance hand; 4 for spring season; 4 for bamboo flower; 4 for winter season. 1 double for triplet of own wind; 1 double for own season; 1 double for own flower.

Double for Concealed Self-Drawn Hand (American and Chinese)

In some games, notably in China and America, a concealed hand is not recognized, although a self-drawn tile can always be given 2 points.

Concealed-self-drawn hand ... 2 points (no extra credit)

Doubles for Groups of Sets (American and Japanese)

Triplets (Japanese): The scores for triplet hands are sometimes raised in popular play. Two alternatives are shown below:

        Four triplets
           1 or 2 concealed   2
           3 concealed   3
           4 concealed .... limit
        Three concealed triplets
           With one sequence   2

Triplets (American): Three concealed triplets is given no special credit. The hands are scored:

        Four triplets
           1, 2 or 3 concealed   1
           4 concealed .... limit
        Three concealed triplets
           With one sequence .... no credit

Fours (Japanese): Officially, fours always count as triplets. In popular play, however, many Japanese score them as follows: A hand containing four fours is a limit hand. Three fours are worth one double. In a hand with one or two fours, they count the same as triplets. No distinction is made between concealed and melded fours in calculating doubles. Americans score four fours as a limit hand, but otherwise count fours as triplets.

1 or 2 fours ...... **same as triplets**

3 fours **1**

4 fours .... **limit**

If the fourth set in a three-fours hand is a sequence, the hand simply receives a double for three fours. But if it is a triplet, the hand also counts as a four-triplets hand, and receives an additional double, making two in all.

EXAMPLE 2: Partially melded hand. Self-drawn tile was 4 character. East round; player is dealer.

M   M   C

$$(20 + 8 + 16 + 16 + 0 + 0 + 2 + 2) \times 2 = 128$$

Each player pays 2×130 to East

20 for winning; 8 for melded four of simples; 16 for melded four of terminals; 16 for concealed four of simples; 0 for sequence; 0 for pair; 2 for self-drawn tile; 2 for one-chance. 1 double for three fours.

Doubles for Ways of Going Out

No additional ways of going out are given doubles except that in the American rules four special limit hands are entitled to doubles. See "The Limit," on page 87.

Doubles for Special Inclusions (Japanese)

The only special inclusion recognized by the Japan Mah Jong Association is the run from one to nine in one suit, which gives a hand one double. Popularly, this score is increased to two doubles if the run is concealed, and many other special inclusions are also scored. All the rules below are in popular usage but none of them appear in the official code.

Three Consecutive Sequences: A run from one to nine in one suit is given one double if the run is partially melded, and two doubles if it is all concealed.

Three consecutive sequences

Partially melded........... 1

All concealed 2

EXAMPLE 3: Concealed hand. Discarded tile, by East, was 5 dot. East round; player is West.

$$(20 + 0 + 0 + 0 + 2 + 2 + 10) \times 4 = 136$$
East pays 4 × 140 to West

20 for winning; 0 for each sequence; 2 for melded triplet of simples; 2 for lucky pair; 10 for concealed hand with discarded tile. 2 doubles for concealed run from 1 to 9.

Three Similar Sequences: If the hand includes three sequences, one of each suit, and all three of the same numbers, it gets one double. It makes no difference whether the sequences are melded or concealed.

Three similar sequences   1

EXAMPLE 4: Concealed hand. Discarded tile, by West, was 9 bamboo. South round; player is South.

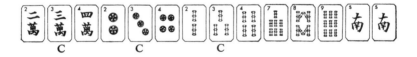

$$(20 + 0 + 0 + 0 + 0 + 4 + 10) \times 2 = 68$$
West pays 4 × 70 to South

20 for winning; 0 for each sequence; 4 for double-wind pair; 10 for concealed hand with discarded tile. 1 double for three similar sequences.

Three Similar Triplets: If the hand includes three triplets, one of each suit, and all three of the same numbers, it gets one double. It makes no difference to this rule whether the triplets are melded or concealed, but if they are all concealed, they score as "three concealed triplets" and get one (or two) additional doubles.

Three similar triplets   1

EXAMPLE 5: Partially melded hand. Discarded tile, by South, was 6 bamboo. South round; player is West.

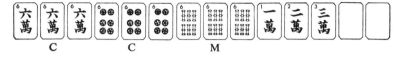

C   C   M

$$(20 + 4 + 4 + 2 + 0 + 2) \times 2 = 64$$
South pays 4 × 60 to West

20 for winning; 4 for concealed triplet of simples; 4 for concealed triplet of simples; 2 for melded triplet of simples; 0 for sequence; 2 for lucky pair. 1 double for three similar triplets.

EXAMPLE 6: Concealed hand. Discarded tile, by South, was 3 character. South round; player is West.

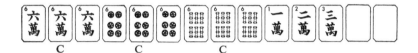

C   C   C

$$(20 + 4 + 4 + 4 + 0 + 2 + 2 + 10) \times 8 = 368$$
South pays 4 × 370 to West

20 for winning; 4 for each concealed triplet of simples; 0 for sequence; 2 for lucky pair; 2 for one-chance; 10 for concealed hand with discarded tile. 1 double for three similar triplets; 2 doubles for three concealed triplets with one sequence.

Note: In the official rules, "three concealed triplets with one sequence" are worth one double, not two.

Two or Three Identical Sequences: Two identical sequences are easy to achieve, and thus receive no credit if they are partially melded. If they are both concealed, they are worth one double. Three identical sequences, which are more difficult to obtain, are worth one double if they are partially melded, and two doubles if all concealed. Usually, however, if they are all concealed, they are more valuable if rearranged to make three concealed triplets. When concealed, they may be displayed as sequences or triplets, but not both. After display, they may not be changed. When melded, of course, they must be scored as they appear on the board.

Two identical sequences	
Melded	**0**
Concealed	**1**
Three identical sequences	
Melded	**1**
Concealed	**2**

EXAMPLE 7: Partially melded hand. Self-drawn tile was 8 dot. East round; dealer.

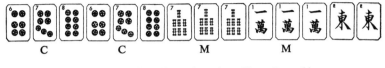

C   C   M   M

$$(20 + 0 + 0 + 2 + 4 + 4 + 2) \times 2 = 64$$
Each player pays 2 × 60 to dealer

20 for winning; 0 for each sequence; 2 for melded triplet of simples; 4 for melded triplet of terminals; 4 for double-wind pair; 2 for self-drawn tile. 1 double for two identical concealed sequences.

EXAMPLE 8: Partially melded hand. Discarded tile, by West, was 7 character. East round; dealer.

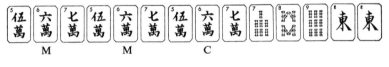

M   M   C

$$(20 + 0 + 0 + 0 + 0 + 4) \times 2 = 48$$
West pays 6 × 50 to dealer

20 for winning; 0 for each sequence; 4 for double-wind pair. 1 double for three identical sequences, partially melded.

Double for No-Points

This is generally the same as described in *Part One* on page 50, although when other scoring rules, like those above, are added, it can be combined with some additional doubles as, for example:

Three similar sequences

Two identical sequences

Three identical sequences

"Ready" declaration

In China and America a no-points hand is allowed to be self-drawn and to have one chance, in which cases the 2 or 4 points ordinarily given are discounted.

Doubles for Consistency

Japan: The only exceptions made by some Japanese players to the rules described in the text are that the two hands "one suit with honors" and "little three dragons," which are officially given one double each, are both raised to two doubles.

One suit with honors **2**
Little three dragons **2**

China and America: The rules very widely, but are predominantly as follows. "All simples" receives no credit.

All simples .... **no credit**

"All terminals and honors" always receives one double, but "terminal or honor in each set" is not recognized.

Terminal or honor in each set .. **no credit**

The one-suit hands are scored:

One suit with honors **1**
One suit only **3**

Finally, wind and dragon hands are defined and scored variously. In America, they are defined as in this text, but scored so that both "little" hands receive one double:

Little three dragons **1**
Big three dragons .... **limit**
Little four winds **1**
Big four winds .... **limit**

In China, the winds hands are defined differently. "Big" and "little four winds" both contain four wind sets, but in "big four winds," the *player's own wind* appears as a *triplet*, while in "little four winds," it is the *pair*. They are then scored as above. Thus in China, a hand containing three triplets of winds, including the player's own, and a pair of the fourth counts as a "big four winds" hand, while in America, as in Japan, it is "little."

Double for "Ready" (Japanese)

If the "ready" declaration is included in the game, a hand that goes out after declaring "ready" receives one double. Many other rules relating to the scoring of "ready" are also popular.

Going out after declaring "ready" ... **1**

EXAMPLE 9: "Ready" hand. Discarded tile, by East, was 2 bamboo. East round; player is South.

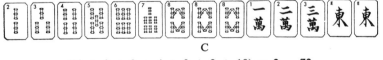

C

$(20 + 0 + 0 + 4 + 0 + 2 + 10) \times 2 = 72$

East pays 4×70 to South

20 for winning; 0 for each sequence; 4 for concealed triplet of simples; 0 for sequence; 2 for lucky pair; 10 for concealed hand with discarded tile. 1 double for "ready."

EXAMPLE 10: "Ready" hand. Self-drawn tile was 2 bamboo. East round; player is South.

C

$$(20 + 0 + 0 + 4 + 0 + 2 + 2) \times 4 = 112$$

Non-dealers pay 110; dealer pays 220

20 for winning; 0 for sequence; 0 for sequence; 4 for concealed triplet of simples; 0 for sequence; 2 for lucky pair; 2 for self-drawn tile. 1 double for "ready" and 1 double for concealed self-drawn hand.

Seven Pairs (Japanese)

No seven-pairs hands are recognized by the Japan Mah Jong Association. Popularly, however, seven pairs is permitted as a winning hand and is scored as follows. It is treated specially with respect to *points*. The score for the hand is always 100 points. The hand then receives doubles if other criteria are met, much as do ordinary hands. Two rules apply to the making of this hand: first, it must of course be concealed. Secondly, no two pairs may be identical. Under all conditions, if you have four of a kind, you must either make a four, or use one of the tiles in a sequence, or discard it.

To score: give the hand 100 points, and then multiply for each double. The following doubles may apply to seven pairs:

> **Going out with last tile of wall**
> **Going out with last discarded tile**
> **Going out by robbing a kong**
> **Going out with a supplement tile**
> **Declaring "ready"**
> **All simples**
> **All terminals and honors**
> **One suit with honors**
> **One suit only** (*Note:* multiplying the 100 points by 16—4 doubles—gives the hand a value above the limit. Thus it is a limit hand, though it is not usually listed as one.)
> **Concealed self-drawn hand**
> **All honors** (*Note:* this is usually made a limit hand. It is almost impossible to achieve, for it must contain one pair of each honor, and thus it deserves the limit.)

American players allow only three seven-pairs hands. See "The Limit," below.

EXAMPLE 11: Concealed hand. Discarded tile, by North, was 1 character. East round; dealer.

100 points; no doubles
North pays 6 × 100 to dealer

EXAMPLE 12: "Ready" hand. Self-drawn tile was 1 character. East round; dealer.

100 × 4 = 400
Each player pays 2 × 400 to dealer
100 points for seven pairs. 1 double for "ready" and 1 double for concealed self-drawn hand.

THE LIMIT

In addition to the ten limit hands defined by the official Japanese rules, many others are popular.

Four Fours (Japanese and American): A hand containing four fours, whether melded or concealed, and no matter what tiles make up the fours, receives the limit.

Four fours: melded or concealed

Seven Pairs (American): Three exceptional seven-pairs hands are defined by the American rules and are given limit scores.
"HEAVENLY TWINS" (1): A seven-pairs hand containing one pair of each honor: East, South, West, North, and the red, green and white dragons. This is a limit hand.

"HEAVENLY TWINS" (2): A seven-pairs hand containing one suit only. This is a limit hand.

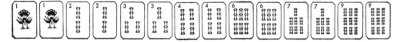

"SEVEN TWINS" A seven-pairs hand containing one suit with honors. This scores half the limit.

> **Seven pairs**
> All honors . . . .   **limit**
> One suit only . . . .   **limit**
> One suit with honors . . . . . $\frac{1}{2}$ **limit**

Note: If these three hands are adopted as defined, they should be the only seven-pairs hands allowed.

Moon from the Bottom of the Sea (Chinese and American): The Chinese and American rules define this as a limit hand. It calls for going out on the last tile of the wall or a subsequent discard, when that tile is 1 dot. *Note:* the Chinese require that this hand be agreed-upon before the game; if it is not, it counts only one double.

The Japanese rules do not distinguish this hand from any other which goes out on the last tile of the wall or a subsequent discard, and credit it with one double only.

Last tile of wall or subsequent discard is 1 dot

Plum Blossom on the Roof (Chinese and American): The Chinese and American rules define this as a limit hand. It calls for going out on a supplement tile, when that tile is 5 dot. *Note:* the Chinese require that this hand be agreed-upon before the game; if it is not, it counts only one double.

The Japanese rules do not distinguish this hand from any other which goes out on a supplement tile, and credit it with one double only.

Supplement tile is 5 dot

Scratching a Carrying Pole (Chinese and American): The Chinese and American rules define this as a limit hand. It calls for going out by robbing a kong, when the tile taken is 2 bamboo. *Note:* the Chinese require that this hand be agreed-upon before the game; if it is not, it counts only one double.

The Japanese rules do not distinguish this hand from any other which goes out by robbing a kong, and credit it with one double only.

Tile robbed from kong is 2 bamboo

Kong on Kong (Chinese and American): The Chinese and American rules define this as a limit hand. It occurs when a player makes a four and draws a supplement tile; this completes a second four and he draws a second supplement tile. The *second* supplement tile completes the hand.

The Japanese rules do not distinguish this from any other hand which goes out on a supplement tile, and credit it with one double only.

Making two fours and going out in one turn

All Green (American): The American rules define as a limit hand one containing the normal four sets and pair, but composed only of green dragons, twos, threes, fours, sixes and eights of bamboo.

The Japanese rules give it no special credit. It is classed as "one suit with honors."

All green tiles

Eighth Extra Hand: This is popular in Japan. If the dealer wins eight successive extra hands, he gets the limit for winning the eighth one, regardless of his hand, even if it is worth only 22 points. This is the *ninth* consecutive hand the dealer has won. The first hand he won was simply his deal; the second was the first extra hand, and so forth.

The hands must all be *won* by the dealer; they may not include redeals after draws.

After the eighth extra hand, the deal passes.

Dealer wins eighth extra hand

PAYING THE WINNER

"Ready" Payment (Japanese)

If the rule of "ready" is used in any of its various forms, a loser who has declared "ready" must forfeit to the winner the 100-point bone he placed on his ready hand. This forfeit is made even if the winner went out on a tile discarded by another player. The 100 points are not doubled for the dealer.

Payment for Dealer's Extra Hand

By the optional rule above, the winner of an extra hand collects 300 points for each ten-point bone displayed by the dealer. These points are shared between the losers if the winner went out self-drawn, and are paid by the discarder of the winning tile if the winner went out on a discard.

The rule greatly affects the game, since these points can become extremely high. In the fourth extra hand, 1200 points are at stake, in addition to the winner's score. For this reason, the payment is not doubled for the dealer.

If the bonus is made a part of the game, players should receive 8000 points initially, and the limit should be raised.

Rounding Off the Score

The Japan Mah Jong Association rules require that the score should be rounded off after the doubles have been applied. 04 is rounded off to 00, and 06 is rounded off to 10. Some other methods are also popular in Japan, and players may wish to adopt them. Whatever way is chosen, it should be used consistently, for the effects of the different methods are significant.

At Payment Time: Suppose a player goes out self-drawn with 2 points and 3 doubles. His score is then $(20 + 2) \times 8 = 176$. Non-dealers will pay him 180. The dealer will pay him (176×2) rounded off to 350. (By the official rules, the dealer pays two times 180, or 360.)

After Adding Points: Suppose a player goes out self-drawn with 18 points and 2 doubles. His point score is taken $(20 + 18 = 38)$ and then rounded off to 40. 40 is then multiplied by 4, and non-dealers pay him 160; the dealer pays 320. (By the official rules, 38 times 4 is rounded off to 150, and he is paid 150 and 300 by the non-dealers and dealer respectively.)

To Nearest Higher Ten: Some players prefer to round off 02 to 10. When this is done, especially in combination with the method in the paragraph above, all scores are raised. It is not advisable, however, for its effect is somewhat unfair, unless rounding off is made the last step in scoring: "at payment time."

CHAPTER FIVE

American Scoring Rules

SETTLEMENT AMONG LOSERS

A variation on scoring, long outdated in Japan, is the American method of the 1930's: having the three losers always pay the winner, even if he goes out on a discarded tile. The losers then settle among themselves for the values of their uncompleted hands. This system is still popular in American Mah Jong, though it might well be dropped, as it unnecessarily delays and complicates the game. For the sake of completeness, however, it is described below.

All three losers pay the winner his entire score, with the dealer receiving or paying double. Then each loser scores his own hand and settles with each of the other losers for the differences between their hands. Losers are allowed to count points only for complete sets, including the pair if they wish, and doubles only for lucky sets, but not for flowers. In these settlements, if the dealer is one of the losers, he receives or pays double the difference between the score of his hand and that of the other losers' hands. The difference is first taken and then rounded off to the nearest ten.

Since the American terminology is somewhat different from that used here, a scoring table is given below.

SCORING TABLE FOR AMERICAN MIXED-HAND GAME

POINTS

Winning 20

Sets
Sequences 0
Triplets "on table" (melded)
    Simples 2
    Terminals or honors 4
Triplets "in hand" (concealed)
    Simples 4
    Terminals or honors 8
Fours "on table" (melded)
    Simples 8
    Terminals or honors 16
Fours "in hand" (concealed)
    Simples 16
    Terminals or honors 32
Pairs
    Dragons of same color..... 2
    Player's own wind........ 2
    Prevailing wind 2
    Player's own wind when
        prevailing 4
Any Flower 4

Last Tile of Hand
Discarded 0
"Winning by draw" (self-drawn) 2
"Filling only place" (one-chance) 2

DOUBLES

Lucky Sets
Lucky triplet or four 1
Double wind triplet or four... 2
Player's own flower 1
Bouquet of four flowers 4

Groups of Sets
Four Triplets ("no sequences")
    1, 2 or 3 concealed 1
    4 concealed ....limit

Ways of Going Out
Last tile of wall 1
Last discarded tile.......... 1
Robbing a kong 1
Supplement tile 1

No-Points ("All Sequences").. 1

Consistency
All terminals and honors 1
One suit with honors 1
One suit only 3
Little three dragons 1
Little four winds 1

For "Ready"
Delayed call 1

SOME OF THE ACCEPTED LIMIT HANDS

Big Three Dragons (Three Great Scholars)
Little Four Winds (Four Small Blessings)
All Honors
All Terminals
Four Concealed Triplets (Hidden Treasure)
Heavenly Hand (Hand from Heaven)
Earthly Hand (Hand from Earth)
Nine Gates
Thirteen Orphans
All Green
Four Fours (All Kongs)
Moon from the Bottom of the Sea
Plum Blossom on the Roof
Scratching a Carrying Pole
Kong on Kong
Seven Pairs, either All Honors, or One Suit Only
    (Heavenly Twins)
Seven Pairs, One Suit with Honors (Seven Twins)
    Note: This is considered to be a half-limit hand.

EXAMPLE: South goes out with a partially melded hand. Discarded tile, by East, was 5 character. East round.

SOUTH

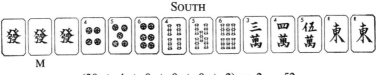

$$(20 + 4 + 0 + 0 + 0 + 2) \times 2 = 52$$

20 for winning; 4 for melded triplet of honors; 0 for each sequence; 2 for lucky pair. One double for lucky set of green dragons.

EAST

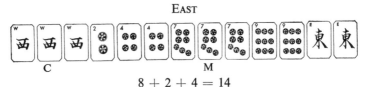

$$8 + 2 + 4 = 14$$

8 for concealed triplet of honors; 2 for melded triplet of simples; 4 for double-wind pair.

WEST

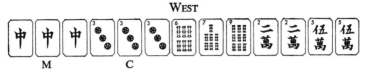

M   C

$$(4 + 4) \times 2 = 16$$

4 for melded triplet of honors; 4 for concealed triplet of simples. 1 double for lucky set of red dragons.

NORTH

C   C

$$(8 + 8) \times 4 = 64$$

8 for each concealed triplet of honors. Two doubles for the two lucky sets: white dragons and own wind.

	East	South	West	North
South collects from the losers.	−100	200	−50	−50
East pays West $(16 - 14) \times 2 = 4$, rounded off to zero.				
East pays North $(64 - 14) \times 2 = 100$.	−100			100
West pays North $(64 - 16) = 48$, rounded off to 50.			−50	50
	−200	200	−100	100

ONE-DOUBLE GAME

Americans sometimes add a rule that a player may not go out with a hand whose score does not include at least one double. The doubles recognized when this rule is in force are the same as in the scoring table above.

Paying the Winner: The winner is paid as in the mixed-hand game, with the dealer receiving or paying double.

Settlement among Losers: The losers settle among themselves as in the mixed-hand game, with a few additional doubles allowed credit. Losers may count the doubles for:

Lucky sets	as above
All terminals and honors	1
One suit with honors	1
One suit only	3
All terminals................	3
All honors	3

This list is only for losers. A winner holding an all-terminals or all-honors hand scores the limit.

The Japanese also sometimes apply the one-double rule, but since they use a simpler system of paying the winner, no additional provisions are needed.

CLEARED-HAND GAME

Another variety of the game sometimes played by Americans is that in which the cleared-hand rule obtains. This restricts the number of permissible winning hands still further, allowing only one-suit hands to go out, with or without honors, the only exceptions being the "all terminals and honors" and "all terminals" hands, and the limit hands, which are allowed to contain more than one suit. The scoring system is the same as that of the mixed-hand game with respect to "points" and "limit hands," but differs with respect to doubles, some of which are reduced to ten points. See the table below.

Paying the Winner: The winner is paid as in the mixed-hand game, with the dealer receiving or paying double.

Settlement among Losers: The losers settle among themselves as in the mixed-hand game, with a few additional doubles allowed credit. Losers may count the doubles for:

Lucky sets	**as above**
All terminals and honors	**1**
One suit with honors	**1**
One suit only	**3**
All terminals...............	**3**
All honors	**3**

This list is only for losers. A winner holding an all-terminals or all-honors hand scores the limit.

DOUBLES IN THE AMERICAN CLEARED-HAND GAME

Points Doubles

Lucky Sets

Lucky triplet or four 1
Double wind triplet or four .. 2
Player's own flower 1
Bouquet of four flowers 4

Groups of Sets

Four triplets
    1, 2 or 3 concealed .. 10
    4 concealed .... limit

Ways of Going Out

Last tile of wall 10
Last discarded tile..... 10
Robbing a kong 10
Supplement tile 10

No-Points(All Sequences) 10

Consistency

All terminals and honors 1
One suit with honors 1
One suit only 3
Little three dragons ... 10
Little four winds 10

Ready

Delayed call 1

PART THREE

Strategy

CHAPTER ONE

Luck and Skill

After playing Mah Jong for a while, one may be tempted to ask, "How can anyone claim that this is a game of skill? You have no control over the draw; you have no clues as to what is coming next. How can skill possibly enter into it at all?" The answer is that Mah Jong does indeed seem to be governed largely—almost entirely—by chance. And it is not precisely skill that is useful, at least not in the sense in which the word is used in chess or *go*. What the Japanese call an *ojōzu* (skillful) player is actually one who knows how to adapt to his luck. This is the whole clue to successful play.

Consider the scoring rules. The highest scores are given to the hands which are least likely to occur—by chance. How can any player, no matter how skillful, cause one of these hands to appear before him? Only by magic? The secret is that the consistent winner in any foursome is very often the player with the lowest average score.

Imagine the following game of Mah Jong. Player A is a "limit-maker"; he tries consistently to make "four concealed triplets," or "thirteen orphans," or "nine gates." Player B is a "one-suit man"; he always makes one-suit hands, usually without honors. Player C is skillful but sleepy. Player D is an expert.

During the game, player A makes two limit hands, and collects a total of 5000 points. Player B makes three one-suit-only hands, and collects about 3000 points. Player C is beset by bad luck, discards carelessly, and loses about 1000 points to each of his opponents. Player D comes out ahead! Why? He wins the remaining sixteen hands with an average score of 70 points each, collecting 4 or 6 times 70 from A, B or C each time. And he never discards the tile that enables another player to go out.

While A has won 5000 points, he has lost almost the same amount, mostly to B and D. While B has won 3000-odd, he has lost it again, mostly to A and D. D has won 5000 and lost only 1500.

The draws are not recorded in the following table, since the players have agreed that the deal will not pass. Counting the dealer's extra hands, there are twenty-five hands of play.

SAMPLE MAH JONG GAME

Round	Hand	Dealer	Winner	Self-drawn	Discarder	Score	Total won	Payments A	B	C	D
I	1	A	A	*		500	3000	+3000	−1000	−1000	−1000
	2	A	D		C	80	320			−320	+320
	3	B	D		A	40	160	−160			+160
	4	C	D		A	40	160	−160			+160
	5	D	D		B	40	240		−240		+240
	6	D	C		A	80	320	−230		+230	
II	7	A	B	*		280	1120	−560	+1120	−280	−280
	8	B	D		A	40	160	−160			+160
	9	C	C		B	40	240		−240	+240	
	10	C	D		A	80	320	−320			+320
	11	D	D		A	80	480	−480			+480
	12	D	D		B	40	240		−240		+240
	13	D	C	*		40	160	−40	−40	+160	−80
III	14	A	B		A	280	1120	−1120	+1120		
	15	B	D		C	240	960			−960	+960
	16	C	D		B	40	160		−160		+160
	17	D	D		B	40	240		−240		+240
	18	D	D		B	40	240		−240		+240
	19	D	B		A	280	1120	−1120	+1120		
IV	20	A	C	*		40	160	−80	−40	+160	−40
	21	B	A		C	500	2000	+2000		−2000	
	22	C	D	*		160	640	−160	−160	−320	+640
	23	D	D		B	40	240		−240		+240
	24	D	D		B	40	240		−240		+240
	25	D	C	*		40	160	−40	−40	+160	−80
					Total won			+5000	+3360	+1040	+5040
					Total lost			−4720	−3360	−4880	−1480
					Final score			+280	0	−3840	+3560

If you examine the table of this imaginary game, you can note the following features of D's play: first, each time he is dealer he wins—with a low score, usually 40. The advantage in this is that as dealer, he receives double his score, so 40 is worth 80 under these circumstances. Naturally his best move is to go out quickly. Of the ten dealer's extra hands, he wins six—each time with a low score. Thus he collects the double, if he is dealer, or prevents someone else's collecting it, if he is not. On two occasions he makes fairly high scores (160, 240), but for the most part he scores 40 points per hand. Most important, he does not discard carelessly. While the other players battle among themselves, winning and losing big scores, player D makes small ones but keeps his gains. Except when a player goes out self-drawn (and in all but the most expert games this happens about quarter of the time), D loses nothing.

The chart shows the results of his playing. But what is his method? The secrets are manifold, but they can be partially summed up in two contradictory statements. First, know the scoring rules backwards and forwards. Second, forget them, because they are seldom useful. In other words, you should be familiar with the big hands, only so that when, once in a blue moon, your dealt hand looks extremely promising, you can make a big score. But in nine hands out of ten, the aim should be to go out fast, relegating the matter of a high score to a place of secondary importance.

What does it avail you, after all, to have all but one of the tiles of a limit hand before you, when your opponent goes out? He collects three hundred points. You would have collected two or three thousand. But you didn't.

In our imaginary game, player D is the silent type, and seems to be utterly unaware of his surroundings. He almost never declares "chow" or "pung," but keeps his hand concealed. Nevertheless, after about seven rounds of discards he is almost invariably ready, and usually goes out about two turns later, with two or three doubles. What wonderful luck! First to have a ready hand shape up so fast—second, to have the last tile he needs appear so soon.

As it turns out, neither of these two things is a matter of chance. The basis of good play, which seems so utterly mysterious to a beginner, is precisely that of making a ready hand early, and making it so that any one of many different tiles will complete it. You can't control the *luck*, but you can control the *likelihood* of its coming your way.

Here are some of the assets of the expert summed up: adaptability, technique for making ready, familiarity with the scoring rules and with the probabilities of the draw, caution in discarding, and quick and penetrating observation of his opponents and their aims. Let us consider them one by one.

Perhaps the most important of all is *adaptability*. A good player accommodates himself to his luck; he doesn't fight it. A poor one gets rattled by bad luck, stubbornly tries to go out in spite of it, takes too many risks, loses to someone else, and gets more rattled. He tends to try persistently to "replay the last hand": whatever went wrong in the previous hand he tries to correct in the present one, failing to realize that the whole situation has changed. Each game is different and requires a different plan of action. And one of the most important aspects of good defensive play is knowing when to give up.

There are three basic sets of tactics for the three basic situations a player faces. First, if you have a good hand from the start, *play to win*. Secondly, if you have a poor hand, *play not-to-lose*, by wary discarding. Thirdly, if you have an utterly hopeless hand, *play for a draw*, by scrapping your hand at the very beginning. A player can sometimes not only avoid losing, but also prevent anyone else's winning.

But that is not all. A hand with splendid prospects may simply not take shape or an apparently hopeless hand may suddenly improve. At every draw you should be ready to change your entire plan.

Another vital feature of good play is making ready. A long section is devoted to this in the following pages. Suffice it to say here that the difference between winning and losing often boils down to nothing more than the ability, or lack of it, to make a ready hand early and well.

Consider the scoring rules and probabilities. First, points. They are not as valuable as they seem. One of the best ways to make a high hand is to start with the double for no-points. To this can be added "all simples," or a run from 1 to 9, or a terminal or honor in each set, and possibly concealed self-drawn hand. This combination gives 20 points and two or three doubles: 80 or 160 points, which is a score well above the average. It is far easier to make than any other hand with that score. Triplets, as compared to sequences, are more difficult to make, and one double is worth twenty points' worth of triplets.

Note: If certain of the alternative scoring rules in *Part Two* are used, this policy is even more advantageous. No-points with a 2-double special inclusion, the "ready" declaration and concealed self-drawn gives 20 points and 5 doubles: 640, which is a score above the limit!

As for the doubles themselves, the more the better of course. Each step up is bigger than the last. Three doubles ($\times$ 8) are better than two by a multiplier of 4; four are better than three by a multiplier of 8, etc. So the best technique, when possible, is to accumulate doubles. Again, the easiest base to start from is that of a hand composed largely or entirely of sequences.

Note: When using the "ready" declaration, if you stay concealed and declare "ready," with any hand, you have a good chance of going out with at least two doubles, one for "ready" and one for "concealed self-drawn." If the hand already contains one or two doubles (for a terminal or honor in each set and one suit with honors, for example), it is nearly a limit hand.

At that point, don't try for more. A hand with 24 or so points and four doubles scores 380, which is well over half the limit, and it is easier to do this twice than to make a limit hand once.

Why so much emphasis on sequences and simples? Because of the probability of drawing them. To make a triplet, you must obtain three out of only four tiles in the set. To make a sequence, you need three out of twelve tiles. This is unlike the deck of cards, in which threes of a kind can be made from the four suits, while runs are made in one suit, and the two are equally likely. The proportion of honors to suit tiles is about one to four, as against one to two in cards, hence honors are far more difficult to collect. Furthermore, suit tiles can be combined into both sequences and triplets, while honors can only be used in triplets. Naturally the player who is clever with the suit tiles has a great advantage over the one who plays with the honors. Finally, the most useful suit tiles are the simples, and of these the most useful, in terms of the probability of drawing and using them, are the ones nearest the middle. A 1 can only be used in a 1-1-1 triplet or in a 1-2-3 sequence. A 2 can be used in a 2-2-2 triplet, a 1-2-3 sequence, or a 2-3-4 sequence. But a 5 can be part of any of the following combinations: 5-5-5, 3-4-5, 4-5-6, 5-6-7. It is on these facts that much of the following material on strategy is based.

Another consideration is that in Mah Jong, unlike most gambling games, *it is not the highest hand but the first hand to go out, that wins.* Under these circumstances, what gambler would fiddle around with honors?

Our expert's other assets are quick observation and caution in discarding. The Japanese say that good health is indispensable to good play in Mah Jong. A good player does not spend the time between turns vacant-minded. Each move of his opponents is a signal to him: "That one is making a hand of bamboo tiles—I must discard them right away or not at all. This one is collecting honors—I'd better keep my pair of red dragons and not try for a one-suit-only hand. That one is looking for a high character tile—I'd better try to make a set of my 6 and 7 characters." Against each player you can use these techniques: watch his face, see if you can guess how he arranges his hand, judge what he's collecting by watching his discards, learn to know how he behaves when he's ready and be especially careful at that time. Spur yourself to making ready ahead of him, so that you can beat him to going out.

Remember also that it is the count of the bones at the end of the game that determines the winner. If you make a limit hand once in every round, that is splendid. But if you are the discarder who must pay four or six times the score of another player when he goes out, and this happens twice in every round, you will probably end up in the hole notwithstanding. To be a winner is good; not-to-be a loser is equally important. Knowing your opponents' hands and discarding wisely are vital to good play. These things are taken up in *Chapter Three*, below, starting on page 139.

I have emphasized low-scoring hands and the use of the simples in order to counteract the prevalent tendency of American players to ignore them and go for "all or nothing," which can be so disastrous in Mah Jong. The emphasis should be modified, however, lest the impression of the imaginary game given above be too strong. Ideally, such a game would never take place. Player D can take tremendous advantage of A and B because they are not strategists. Player C, for purposes of illustrating a point, was made "sleepy." But in a game with four good players, high scores have more meaning, and an occasional big hand can turn the tide of the game decisively to one player's favor. When all four are good players, each plays to win each hand, and to win it with the highest possible score. It is still the player who goes out first that collects, but if he cannot capitalize on whatever opportunities arise, he may lose in the end.

In other words, ultimately every good player should think of everything. He should know how to estimate the hand he is dealt, and how to look ahead and plan; he should recognize the elements of sets and be familiar with their potentialities; he should know how and when to make combinations, and what tiles are safe to discard at what times. He should estimate shrewdly the characters of his opponents and play accordingly. He should know when to go out with a low score, and when to try for a high-scoring hand or for the limit. The next two chapters are devoted to these techniques.

CHAPTER TWO
Offensive Strategy

ARRANGEMENT OF THE HAND

A skillful player does not arrange his hand. A quick glance is all he needs to tell him what it contains and how he should play it. If you do arrange it, however, the following "don'ts" may be useful.

Don't keep honors on the right side. When playing fast, you may accidentally expose them.

Don't separate the tiles of your hand into groups. Your opponents can draw too many conclusions about your progress from this.

Don't try to maintain a very systematic arrangement during the game. You should constantly be watching your opponents and their discards, keeping in mind the contents of your hand. You can too easily miss an important move.

Don't arrange in the same way every time. An observant player will be quick to learn your system and deduce your plans and progress from watching where you put the tiles you draw.

Don't forget to keep a discard ready for each two-tile element, as explained below. It may be wise to keep each discard next to the element with which you associate it.

ELEMENTS

Japanese books on Mah Jong list exhaustively the elements of sets and give a name to each of them. It is not necessary, however, to memorize all of them in order to be a good player, if you understand the principles involved in dealing with them. The idea is to recognize the potentialities of each element or group of suit tiles, and to be able to estimate its value.

Every group of three or more number tiles is a combination of the five basic elements listed below:

One Tile (Example: 2) This is a potential pair. **Three** remaining tiles out of the set will match it. It is the worst of all the elements.

Serial Pair (Example: 2-3) This can become a sequence with either a 1 or a 4. Any one of **eight** tiles will complete it. This is the best two-tile element.

Terminal Serial Pair (Example: 1-2) This can become a sequence only with a 3 and therefore is not very hopeful. One of **four** tiles will complete it.

Separated Pair (Example: 2-4) This can become a sequence only with a 3. It is as bad as the terminal serial pair since only one of **four** tiles will complete it.

Pair (Example: 2-2) This can be the pair of the hand, as it stands. Or another 2 will make a triplet. This is the least hopeful two-tile element for a set of three because only one of **two** remaining tiles will complete it.

The three-tile elements are judged similarly. The more chances there are to complete them, the better they are. The best has ten chances; the worst has four. Recognizing their value is an important part of skillful play. There are four types of three-tile elements for number tiles that call for attention.

a) Serial Pair With Matching Tile (Example: 2-2-3) Another 2 will make a triplet. A 1 or 4 will make a sequence. Four 1's, four 4's and two 2's are left in the set. Thus any one of **ten** tiles will complete it. This is the best three-tile element.

b) Terminal Serial Pair With Matching Tile (Example: 1-1-2) A 1 will make a triplet. A 3 will make a sequence. Two 1's and four 3's remain in the set. Thus any one of **six** tiles will complete this element.

c) Separated Pair With Matching Tile (Example: 2-2-4) A 2 will make a triplet; a 3 will make a sequence. Two 2's and four 3's remain in the set. Thus any one of **six** tiles will complete it.

d) Three Consecutive Odd or Even Numbers (Example: 1-3-5) This will make a sequence with a 2 or with a 4. There are **eight** remaining tiles any one of which will complete it.

Note that d) is a more hopeful element than b) and c) above, although it does not look so valuable. However, a), b) and c) are more useful in another sense: if you have the option of using the included pair as it is, it is a complete set, while element d) is worthless as it stands.

Other combinations, such as 2-3-5 or 1-2-4, should not be counted as three-tile elements. In both of these cases, one tile is not related to the other two. In 2-3-5, for example, you are waiting for a 4 in any case and either the 2 or the 5 will not form part of your completed set. This does not mean, however, that the extra tile should not be kept. A sequence of four, as explained below, is useful for a ready hand.

Of the groups of four or more tiles, it is necessary only to remember this general rule: consecutive tiles are usually better than matching ones. In analyzing them, recognize the two-tile elements in them, and you can easily estimate their value. Two special groups are very useful:

Sequence of Four (Example: 2-3-4-5) Remember to look at this as two serial pairs: -2-3- and -4-5-. To the beginner it looks like a sequence with an extra tile. But it can easily become two sequences, with a 1 or 4 and a 3 or 6. It is also a useful asset for making ready. If your other sets are complete, you can use it to make a sequence and the pair. Either a 2 or 5 will make the pair, and the remaining three tiles will be a complete sequence. Thus any tile from 1 to 6 is useful: 20 tiles in all. This is an excellent group.

Sequence of Five (Example: 2-3-4-5-6) Do not make the mistake of breaking this up into a sequence and serial pair. It will make two sequences in any one of three ways: with a 1, a 4 or a 7. (1 makes 1-2-3, 4-5-6; 4 makes 2-3-4, 4-5-6; 7 makes 2-3-4, 5-6-7.) A 2, 3, 5 or 6 will leave you with a complete sequence and the best of the three-tile elements: a serial pair with matching tile. For example, 2 will make 2-2-3 and 4-5-6. The 2-2-3 group can then be completed by 1 or 2 or 4.

The following examples will illustrate the value of thinking in terms of elements, and demonstrate some of the techniques involved in dealing with them.

EXAMPLE 1: 5-6-6

Beginner discards the 5, and waits for a 6—and there are only two 6's left in the set.

Expert keeps all three, waits for a 4 or 7 to make a sequence, or for a 6. Ten tiles still left in the set will complete the group. If he must discard one, he discards a 6 and waits for a 4 or 7—and there are four of each left in the set.

EXAMPLE 2: 3-4-4-5

Beginner discards a 4 and makes a 3-4-5 sequence.

Expert keeps all four tiles unless he has four other good elements or sets in his hand. This group is potentially two sequences: -3-4- and -4-5-. He waits for a 2 or 5 to complete the first one, and for a 3 or 6 to complete the other. The group can also become a sequence and pair, with another 4.

EXAMPLE 3: 2-3-4-5

Beginner discards a 2 or 5 and keeps the sequence.

Expert keeps all four tiles and waits to draw some more from the wall. This run is potentially two sequences: -2-3- and -4-5-; it is also potentially one sequence and a pair: 2-3-4 and 5-5, or 2-2 and 3-4-5. If he wants two sequences, he waits for a 1 or 4 and for a 3 or a 6. If he wants a sequence and a pair, he waits for a 2 or 5. Thus any tile from 1 to 6 will substantially increase his chances of going out.

EXAMPLE 4: Player holds 1-2-3-3; someone discards a 3.

Beginner says "pung," melds 3-3-3, and then must discard the 1 and 2 which are no longer useful. He has made a set of three and acquired 2 points and two useless tiles.

Expert says nothing. He discards one of his 3's later on, because he knows it is safe and keeps the 1-2-3 sequence. He thus has a set of three and a safe discard.

EXAMPLE 5: Player holds 2-3-4-4; someone discards a 4.

Beginner says "pung," melds 4-4-4, and then waits for a 1 or 4 to complete his sequence. But only one 4 is left in the set, and most of the 1's have probably been discarded early. His chances are slim.

Expert says "pung" only if he can make ready, waiting for 1 or 4 as above. Otherwise, he keeps quiet, discards his own 4 later on, because he knows it is safe and keeps the 2-3-4 sequence. See also: "Making the Pair," example 26, on page 120.

EXAMPLE 6: What should be discarded?

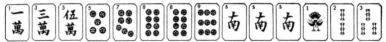

There are five possible discards: 1 character, 5 character, 5 dot, 8 dot and 9 dot. The triplet of South and sequence of 1-2-3 bamboo are complete, so the hand needs two additional sets of three and a pair. Considering each discard in turn, you should ask what tiles you would need, and how many chances you have to draw them, and base your decision on the answer.

Discarding 1 character, you will need 4 character (4 chances) to make 3-4-5 character. You will need 5 dot or 8 dot to make 5-5 and 7-8-9 dot, or 8-8 and 7-8-9 dot (5 chances). This alternative gives **9 chances** to draw the two tiles needed.

Discarding 5 character has the same effect as discarding 1 character, and gives **9 chances**.

Discarding 5 dot, you will need either 2 or 4 character (8 chances), to make a character sequence. Then either the isolated character or an 8 dot can be used for the pair, in which case you need either 1 or 5 character or 8 dot for which you have 8 chances. This alternative gives **16 chances** to draw the two tiles needed.

Discarding 8 dot has the same effect as discarding 5 dot. The pair can then be 1-1 or 5-5 character or 5-5 dot (9 chances) and the sequence can be either 1-2-3 or 3-4-5 character (8 chances). This alternative gives **17 chances** to draw the two tiles needed.

Discarding 9 dot, you will need either 2 or 4 character (8 chances) to make a sequence, and 6 dot to make another sequence (4 chances). 8-8 dot can be used as the pair. This alternative gives **12 chances** to draw the two tiles needed.

Keep 1-3-5 character complete, until you draw a 1, 2, 4 or 5. Discard either 5 or 8 dot, whichever is safer.

EXAMPLE 7: What should be discarded?

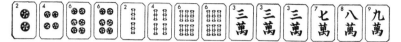

There are four possible discards: 2 dot, 2 bamboo, 6 dot, or 6 bamboo. The two character sets are complete, so the hand needs two additional sets of three and a pair. The decision should be made on the same basis as in Example 6 above. Since the dot and bamboo groups are identical, discarding a 2 from either will have the same effect; discarding a 6 from either will also have the same effect. Let us consider only the dot group.

Discarding 2 dot commits you to the use of 6-6 bamboo as the pair. You then need 3 bamboo (4 chances) to make a sequence, and either 5 or 6 dot (6 chances) to make 4-5-6 or 6-6-6 dot. This alternative gives **10 chances** to draw the two tiles needed.

Discarding 6 dot has the same effect. You need 3 bamboo (4 chances) and either 3 or 5 dot (8 chances) to make 2-3-4 or 4-5-6 dot. This gives a total of **12 chances** to draw the two tiles needed.

Discard either 6 dot or 6 bamboo, whichever is safer. Since the difference between the alternatives, 6 and 2, is slight, you should consider discarding a 2, if 6 is a risky discard.

LOOKING AHEAD

Judging the Dealt Hand

The first thing you should do, when you look at your hand, is figure out how many tiles you need to go out. Recognize the elements of sets described above; visualize the completed sets, and count the number of tiles you need to draw. Your beginning setup should determine your plan for the game.

A good general rule is that if you need only **four tiles**, or fewer, you can expect to be ready in less than nine turns. Play to win. If you need **five tiles**, your luck should determine how you play. With good draws, you could be ready early; with bad draws, you will have to give up. If you need **six or more tiles**, give up immediately. Try to make ready if you can, but play defensively in the main.

EXAMPLE 8

Visualize the simplest possibility of developing this into a winning hand:

Note how many tiles are needed: 1 or 4 dot; 3 or 6 (or 5) character; 1 or 4 bamboo; and 4 or 7 bamboo. The pair is already complete. If you draw another red dragon, you can make 5-5 character the pair.

This is an excellent dealt hand. You need only **four tiles**. You should be ready in about seven or eight turns, and should be able to go out in nine or ten.

EXAMPLE 9

Visualize the simplest possibility of developing this into a winning hand:

Note how many tiles are needed: 3 or 6 character; 6 or 9 bamboo; 2 tiles to make a set from 2 dot or 8 character or 1 or 4 bamboo; and 1 tile to complete a pair.

This is a fairly good hand. You need **five tiles**. With good luck you can make ready within ten turns, but with bad luck, you can not. Be adaptable; be prepared to go out low or to give up. Play defensively.

EXAMPLE 10

Visualize the simplest possibility of developing this into a winning hand:

Note how many tiles are needed: 8 character; 3 dot; 4 tiles to complete each of two additional sets; 1 tile to complete a pair.

This is a poor hand. You need **seven tiles** in all, a hopeless outlook. You cannot be ready even with perfect luck, before the sixth turn; so you probably could not make ready with average luck, until about the fifteenth. Give up now and play defensively.

Planning

Playing to Win: If you need only a few tiles to make ready, play boldly. Capitalize on your luck while it lasts. Discard anything you don't need at the beginning; don't hesitate even to discard lucky tiles. After six or seven draws, if your luck is holding, feel free to say "chow" or "pung" in order to make ready early. Of course, you should keep your hand concealed if you can, and remember to watch your opponents. A discard in the fourth or fifth round of play may be dangerous even if you are already ready. But it is seldom that two players both make ready within the first six turns.

Playing Not to Lose: A dealt hand which needs five tiles usually calls for this policy. Try to balance offensive and defensive techniques by discarding with caution right from the start while trying simultaneously to make a ready hand. This is difficult to do, and should soon be resolved into a definite yes-or-no procedure. After about four draws from the wall, it should be clear what your chances are. If you now need only three tiles, play to win. If you need four or more, play for a draw.

Playing for a Draw: This is analogous to the technique of stalemating in chess; if you cannot win, you do not necessarily have to lose. If one player is completely uncooperative, discarding nothing which will be useful to his opponents, he can sometimes singlehandedly bring the game to a draw, without anyone's going out.

First, discard with great caution. This is the most important element in playing for a draw. Do not be the first to discard any dragon or wind except your own. Don't play with doubles; you will find yourself collecting honors because they are not safe discards, but if you have a pair of them in your hand and someone discards one, don't claim it for a triplet. Now you know it is safe to discard them immediately.

Second, keep the hand concealed. In other words, almost never say "chow" or "pung." That way, you always have thirteen tiles, from which to choose a safe discard.

Third, keep your intent concealed from your opponents. One of the most effective ways to bring a hand to a draw is by making your adversaries believe that you are close to going out with a big score. This can be done by clever discarding, and by subtle behavior. The section on "Deduction and Psychology" at the end of *Chapter Three*, page 146, includes some hints.

Anticipating Discards

The order of precedence in discarding will be covered more completely in the chapter on "Defensive Strategy," below. It should be noted, however, that when first dealt a hand, a player should consider the elements he intends to complete, partially from the point of view of the discards he will make. Occasionally, this may call for a special procedure with respect to the precedence of discards.

Remember that for each two-tile element you must have one discard. For each one-tile element you must have two—one for the occasion when you draw a tile connected with the first—and a second discard when you complete the set. Thus, attempting to hold two single lucky tiles (one of the beginner's most common mistakes) obligates you, immediately or eventually, to discard four tiles from the remainder of your hand. On the other hand each three-tile element includes a "natural" discard. For example, when you draw a 3 to 4-4-5, you can discard the 4; when you draw a 6 to 5-7-9, you can discard the 9.

In every dealt hand, one should recognize, not only the elements but also the discards that will be made as each element becomes a set. In the event that an element itself will eventually have to be discarded, this anticipation is particularly important, since discarding it may be dangerous if postponed.

Recognizing Potential Doubles

Every player wants to make a high score if possible. But this should not be attempted unless the elements for a high-scoring hand are already present at the beginning. Following are some typical dealt hands, with suggested playing techniques for each of the most common ones, ranging from a low score to the maximum. The Japanese text books on Mah Jong list them as the minimum requirements for each of the corresponding hands.

Hopeless Hand: Do not fail to recognize this. One of the worst mistakes a beginner makes is attempting to go out with a hand that has no winning potential. Three examples are given below. Play for a draw, with this hand.

EXAMPLE 11

The hand has three elements:
  a) 4-5 bamboo needs one of a possible eight tiles to make a sequence.
  b) 5-7 character needs one of a possible four tiles for a sequence.
  c) 9-9 dot is a complete pair.

In addition, the hand needs at least four tiles to make two additional sets. Thus it needs **six tiles** in all. Play defensively from the beginning, and do not try to go out. Never discard the red and white dragons; discard East and North only immediately after someone else does. Play for a draw.

EXAMPLE 12

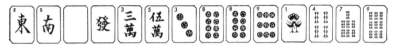

The hand has three elements:
    a) 3-5 character needs one of a possible four tiles to make a sequence.
    b) 8-8-9 dot needs one of a possible six tiles to make a sequence or triplet (either 7 to make 7-8-9 or 8 to make 8-8-8).
    c) 7-9 bamboo needs one of a possible four tiles to make a sequence.
At least two additional tiles are needed for another set, and one more for the pair: thus, **six tiles** in all. The hand is hopeless. Discard 1 bamboo and hope for lucky tiles in the draw to match your dragons, but play for a draw unless your luck is extraordinarily good.

EXAMPLE 13

The hand has two elements:
    a) 8-9 dot needs one of a possible four tiles to make a sequence.
    b) 5-7 bamboo needs one of a possible four tiles to make a sequence.
The other tiles have no relation to one another, so at least five additional tiles will be needed, or **seven tiles** in all. Give up immediately and play for a draw.

A Few Lucky Tiles and Miscellaneous Suit Tiles: Make ready soon, if possible. Don't play with doubles. Go out as quickly as you can, even if your score will be very low.   **Low hand**

EXAMPLE 14

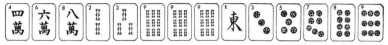

The hand has five elements:

 a) 4-6-8 character needs one of eight possible tiles to make a sequence.
 b) 2-3 bamboo needs one of eight possible tiles to make a sequence.
 c) 9-9-9 bamboo is a complete triplet.
 d) 3-5-7 dot needs one of eight tiles to make a sequence.
 e) 8-8 dot can be the pair.

The hand needs only **three tiles**, but the elements are not ideal. East should be discarded immediately. The character group should be kept intact; if a 5 is drawn, the 8 can be discarded, or if a 7 is drawn, the 4 can go. The 3-5-7 dot group should be treated similarly. Use 8-8 dot as the pair unless you draw a 9 to make 7-8-9; then you can choose between discarding an 8 dot or a 9 bamboo.

The hand has no flexibility, because the elements are large and unwieldy. If you draw 1 or 4 bamboo early, you will have to discard a dot or character tile; judge from the other players' discards and melds which is the least likely to be useful. Bad luck could be ruinous to this hand.

One Lucky-Tile Pair and Miscellaneous Suit Tiles: Make ready soon, if possible. Try to get one double by making a triplet of the lucky tiles, but be reconciled to using them as the pair if the hand has no other available pair. Go out as quickly as you can.   **Average hand**

EXAMPLE 15

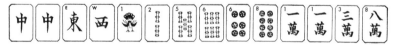

The hand has five elements:

 a) 1-2 bamboo needs one of four tiles to make a sequence.
 b) 5-6 bamboo needs one of eight tiles to make a sequence.
 c) 6-8 dot needs one of four tiles to make a sequence.
 d) 1-1-3 character can be the pair (1-1) as it stands, or needs one of four tiles to make a sequence (2 to make 1-2-3).
 e) The two red dragons can be the pair as they stand, or need one of two tiles for a triplet.

The hand needs only **four tiles** to go out, but the elements are not ideal. 1-2 bamboo is the hardest set to complete, because 3's are always hard to get, and if it fails to appear, you will have to give up. If you draw 3 bamboo soon, feel free to discard either East or West, but your first discard should be 8 character. Keep both the sequence- and pair-possibilities open for the character group; they may be useful as a pair if you can make a lucky set of red dragons.

Only Four (or Fewer) Terminals or Honors, and Miscellaneous Suit Tiles: Try to eliminate all terminals and honors in order to get one double. Keep no-points in mind for another double, but don't be too ambitious. Better to win with one double than to lose with two. **All simples**

EXAMPLE 16

The hand has five or six elements:
  a) 3-4 character needs one of eight tiles to make a sequence.
  b) 4-5 bamboo needs one of eight tiles to make a sequence.
  c) 7-8 bamboo needs one of eight tiles to make a sequence.
  d) 3-5-5-5 dot needs one of four tiles to make a sequence and pair, or can be a complete triplet.
  e) 9-9 dot can be the pair.

This is one of the hands that is overloaded with elements. One of them will have to be discarded; the apparently obvious first choice is 3 dot. The hand would then consist of three sequences, a triplet, and a pair. However, a better choice of discard is the pair of 9 dots. If these and North are eliminated from the hand, it will receive two doubles, for all simples and no-points.

Don't discard 3 dot because with the 5 dot group it is necessary for a sequence and pair. Discard North immediately, and if you complete 3-4 character, 4-5 bamboo and 7-8 bamboo early and have no other terminals, discard 9-9 dot and wait for 4 dot to make a two-double winning hand. But if you draw 9 bamboo instead of 6 bamboo and must make a terminal sequence of 7-8-9, or if the drawing is slow, be reconciled to going out with a lower score.

Four or More Serial Pairs or Other Sequence Elements: Make four sequences, which should be easy, and make no triplets. If you happen to get a pair, keep it for the pair of the hand, and discard the third member if you draw it. It is better to work from serial pairs than from separated oɪ terminal serial pairs, because they are more readily completed. Improve your elements as you go. For example, if you are keeping 3-5 (waiting for 4) and you draw a 6, keep 5-6 (waiting for 4 or 7) and discard the 3, if necessary.

Don't declare "chow." Suit tiles grow naturally into sequences. A melded set loses connections which might be useful later. Given the elements, this is the easiest hand to make. It should be possible to keep it concealed, and even to go out by drawing from the wall for an extra double, especially if you make ready with many chances.

Keep "all simples" in mind and also the run from 1 to 9, but don't be too ambitious.   **No-points**

EXAMPLE 17

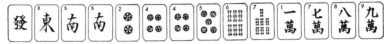

The hand has four elements:
   a) 2-4-4-5 dot needs two of eight tiles to make two sequences.
   b) 6-7 bamboo needs one of eight tiles for one sequence.
   c) 7-8-9 character is a complete sequence.
   d) South-South is a complete pair.
The hand needs **three tiles** in all. It should be ready very early. If South is not a lucky tile, try for no-points, with 2-3-4 dot, -4-5- (with 3 or 6) dot, -6-7- (with 5 or 8) bamboo, 7-8-9 character and South-South as the sets. Discard 1 character immediately, and discard East and the green dragon as soon as anyone else does.

Three or Four Pairs, with a Sequence Element, and Lucky Draws: Usually, this hand would be considered as having *a few lucky tiles and miscellaneous suit tiles*, as described a few pages back, but if the first few draws convert your pairs into triplets, you have a chance of making three concealed triplets. Don't say "pung," until at least the second discard of the tile you need. When the triplets are completed, you can make ready waiting to complete the sequence or pair, so that you are free to go out on a discarded tile.

It is almost impossible to make four triplets of this hand. Don't try, unless you have extraordinary good luck. Don't destroy the sequence element until the very end, if at all.   **Three concealed triplets**

EXAMPLE 18

Four or Five Pairs: Four-triplets hands are supposedly typical of "country Mah Jong," but they are good if you can make them. The points for each of the triplets are doubled, and the hand is often likely to include one or more high-scoring fours before you have finished. But you must have at least four pairs and preferably five to begin with. You will probably have to say "pung," but consider waiting for the second discard of the tile before doing so. **Four triplets**

EXAMPLE 19

Four or Five Pairs and Lucky Draws: Usually this hand is good for four triplets, or at best, three concealed triplets. But if you can make ready with a concealed hand and go out self-drawn, or if you make ready with four concealed triplets and wait for the pair, you will get the limit.

Four concealed triplets
Four triplets with three concealed

EXAMPLE 20

Five or Six Pairs: If you are dealt six pairs, or if you are dealt five and draw another immediately, you must plan carefully. One of the pairs will have to be discarded, since the hand is a natural *four-concealed-triplets* hand. The best to discard is a pair of simples, since this is likely to be the hardest to complete, but it should be done immediately, or it will be too dangerous. **Four concealed triplets**

Note: If seven pairs is agreed upon as a winning hand, and you have six pairs immediately after the start of the game, try to make it, but if you have four to five pairs, *four triplets* is usually better, anyway. Making seven pairs is difficult, and the score is not very high. The ready hand is usually late, and you must make ready with only one chance to go out. However, since the hand must remain concealed, it is often, though not always, a good idea to declare "ready," if it is allowed, and double the score.

Sometimes seven pairs simply do not materialize. Be ready to give up. Once having decided to make the hand and having collected six pairs, however, be cautious about changing your mind and making triplets. Discards are hard to choose from a hand like this unless they are obvious from other players' previous discards. **Seven pairs**

Five Elements, Each Including a Terminal or Honor, with Fewer than Four Simples Between 3 and 6: Composing triplets of honors, and terminal sequences, is more difficult than making middle number sequences. You should have the element for every set from the beginning. Discarding middle simples is dangerous, so do it immediately. Keep 3's and 7's (and 2's and 8's) for terminal sequences until you are sure you won't need them. Declare "chow" or "pung" if necessary. But be prepared to give up.

Terminal or honor in each set

EXAMPLE 21

Five Pairs of Terminals and Honors: Only with this kind of dealt hand can you plan the high-scoring hand of terminals and honors. It is worth a few risks if you have this starting material, so go ahead and declare "pung" if a tile you need appears. Remember, if you meld two triplets of terminals or honors, your opponents will begin to be very cautious with their discards, so calculate carefully whether you should say "pung."

All terminals and honors

EXAMPLE 22

Two or More Pairs of Lucky Tiles and Some Suit Elements: Keep the pairs of lucky tiles for two triplets or triplet and pair, and collect only one suit of tiles, whichever is the most promising. If, before discarding the other two suits you collect a sequence in one of them, hesitate. It is better to go out with a low hand than to lose with a high one. If you decide to persist, don't discard the sequence all at once, or your plan will be obvious. Don't collect isolated dragons and winds in the hope that you can make additional honor sets; this is almost never possible. In your suit tiles, favor sequences over triplet elements; they combine much more readily.

Melding of any of the suit tiles is very unwise. If connections between the sets are broken, it may easily become impossible to make a ready hand.

Melding honor sets does not decrease the chances of making a ready hand, but serves to alert your opponents.

In any case, given the initial elements, this is not a difficult hand to make, and even if you cannot make ready early, you should keep in mind the fact that a comparatively late ready hand with many chances is as good as an early one with few.   **One suit with honors**

EXAMPLE 23

Nine or More Tiles of One Suit: To make a one-suit-only hand, you must start with an absolute minimum of eight tiles of one suit, and it is highly advisable to start with nine or ten. If you are quite sure that you can make the hand, discard lucky tiles early, because they will be dangerous later. Otherwise, try one suit with honors. If you draw lucky tiles late, change to one suit with honors.

Don't make triplets or fours, especially melded ones, unless it is unavoidable, for this will cut the connections between your tiles and is likely to make a good ready hand impossible. In the first few turns, don't make melded sequences either, for the more tiles you have concealed, the better the ready hand you can make. With reasonably good luck in the draw, you should be able to make a four- or five-chance ready hand in about ten turns.

Don't forget the nine-gates limit hand, but don't go out of your way for it. It will either happen or it won't, although you can try to keep the possibility open.   **One suit only**
Nine gates

EXAMPLE 24

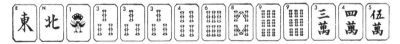

Ten or More Different Terminals and Honors: This is utterly hopeless unless good draws give you additional terminals and honors. Try the special limit hand. Except with extraordinarily good luck, you can complete this hand only if you start with ten of the necessary tiles. Play boldly. A special technique is advisable with respect to discards: discard the most dangerous (the middle number) suit tiles first, and save the safer discards for later.   **Thirteen orphans**

EXAMPLE 25

Making the Pair

As becomes obvious with experience, one of the most important single factors in expert play is making an early and many-chance ready hand. In order to do this, you must remember to provide for the pair early, so that you will not have to make ready waiting for a single tile. Remember, a late pair means a late or poor ready hand, and the ready hand is the key to going out. A few examples will illustrate good technique.

EXAMPLE 26: The player on your left discards a 3 dot.

Beginner says "pung," melds 3-3-3, and waits for the single remaining 3 to complete a 2-3-4 sequence.

Expert says "chow," melds 2-3-4, and keeps 3-3 for the pair. He looks at the group in terms of elements: -2-3- and -3-4-, or 2-4 and -3-3-, and recognizes the pair as an important set just as it is.

EXAMPLE 27: You draw a 5 bamboo.

Beginner keeps the triplet of 3's, discards either 4 or 5 bamboo, and waits for a single tile.

Expert discards a 3 character and keeps 3-3 character as the pair. He looks at 4-5 bamboo as a much easier element to complete than 4 bamboo alone. While only three available tiles will complete the beginner's hand, eight will complete the expert's.

EXAMPLE 28: You draw a 2 bamboo (or 4, or 1, or 5).

Beginner discards the drawn tile. Continues to wait for East. He has, at best, three chances to draw it.

Expert discards East, if it is safe. Keeps 2-3-3-3 bamboo, and looks at it this way: -2-3-, 3-3. Waits for 1 or 4 bamboo. He has eight chances to draw what he needs, and has provided for his pair.

EXAMPLE 29: Someone discards a green dragon.

This is a lucky tile, so you should declare "pung," unless it is late in the game and you have no chance of subsequently going out. The double acquired from the lucky set is too valuable to ignore.

Beginner declares "pung," melds triplet of green dragons, discards 3 or 5 dot and waits with the other dot tile for the pair.

Expert declares "pung," melds triplet of green dragons, discards 3 or 5 dot. Now his opponents know that near neighbors in the dot suit are dangerous. Realizing this, on his next draw he discards the other dot tile, and waits with his new tile for the pair. This is an unfortunate ready hand, but at least no one will have any clue as to what he is waiting for.

EXAMPLE 30: You are ready, waiting for 1 or 4 character, but it is late in the game. You draw a red dragon, which is not safe to discard. What should you do?

Beginner can't bear to give up his ready hand. Holds his breath and discards red dragon anyway. He may get away with it, but he probably won't. Someone almost invariably declares "pung," and melds the set of lucky tiles, often making ready by doing so. Subsequently this player goes out with an extra double for his lucky set, and the beginner must pay for his blunder. It also often happens that by this time a player is ready, waiting with two pairs, and the lucky tile completes his hand.

Expert keeps the red dragon, and destroys one of the other sets, whichever is safer to discard. For example, he destroys 2-3 character, and is reconciled to giving up and playing for a draw. He does not give up entirely, however, but plans this way: if someone discards 9 character, he will declare "pung," meld the 9 character triplet, and discard the other character tile, waiting with the red dragon for the pair. If he draws a red dragon, he will discard the other character tile and wait either for a third red dragon or a third 9 character to go out.

MAKING READY

The key to successful play, as explained above, is making ready. It is important to grasp the concepts involved, for it is the clever "ready-maker" who goes out most often and thus makes the highest score.

To make ready means to prepare to go out. The way in which this is done determines the number of chances you will have to go out. The beginner tends to complete his four sets of three and then try to match his last tile to make the pair. He may draw and draw and draw without getting the tile he needs. The expert is more likely to make ready in such a way that any one of three or more different kinds of tiles will complete his hand. Then he is almost sure to draw one of the tiles that will do.

The simplest way to learn the technique is this: at the beginning of the game do not decide too definitely how your hand will be completed. Simply collect simples, preferably of only one or two suits, and let them arrange themselves. Make no melds. You will find that your tiles fall naturally into groups. Watch carefully and you will recognize situations in which your hand has become ready "all by itself." The only difference between this method and expert play is that the expert can foresee the likely combinations and guide his hand toward them to a degree.

A little experience and a lot of thought will make you a good judge of ready-hand possibilities.

Ready Techniques

It is good to make ready early, but more important to have many chances to go out. A late ready hand with many chances is usually better than an early one with one chance. Ideally, however, the ready hand should be in accordance with all of the following:

Within Six or Seven Turns: If you are not ready by the tenth round of discards, you should consider giving up. By the fourteenth round of play, you are in great danger if you continue to try to make ready and fail to play defensively. Very skillful players often make ready within four or five turns, given good luck in drawing.

Concealed: People can not tell if your hand is ready, or, with any great accuracy, what tiles you are waiting for, if your hand is concealed. Also, with thirteen tiles in your hand, you can often make improvements and changes, while remaining ready.

Many Chances to Go Out: The more the better. The various kinds of ready hands are listed below. It is sometimes possible to wait for six or seven or even more different tiles to complete your hand.

Waiting for Easy-to-Discard Tiles: Players go out by using someone else's discarded tile three or four times as often as by drawing. So, if possible, plan your hand so that you will be waiting for suit tiles near 1 or 9. For example, holding 7-7-7-8, waiting for 8 or 9, is better than 4-5-5-5, waiting for 3 or 4, because 8 and 9 are more likely to be discarded. It is highly advisable to wait for tiles already showing on the board, for all players avoid discarding "new" tiles after the first few turns.

In general, when composing your hand, keep "ready" in mind. Don't try to make individual sets; try to make ready. For example:

Given 3-4-5, if you draw a 6, don't discard it. Keep all four tiles. When the other three sets are complete, you will be ready, waiting for 3 or 6.

Given 3-4-5-6, if you draw a 7, keep that too. When you have made two other sets and the pair, you will be ready, waiting for 2, 5 or 8.

Given neighboring triplets, for example three 4's and three 5's, if you draw a 6, don't discard it. When you have made two other sets, you will be ready, waiting for 4, 5, 6 or 7.

Given a hand with one complete triplet, 2-3-4-5-6 bamboo, 6-7-8 character and two isolated tiles, if you draw 5 character, keep it, and discard an isolated tile. Now a 5 or 8 character, or a 1, 4 or 7 bamboo will make your hand ready with two or three chances.

With experience, you will learn to recognize a hand that is one or two "steps before ready." The Japanese have special names for these. You should then be able to recognize how many chances you have to take the next step. The last hand above is two steps before ready.

EXAMPLE 31

This hand is very nearly complete: it is one step before ready. How many different tiles will make it ready? The player who can recognize this ahead of time will have the presence of mind to say "chow" or "pung" if necessary, when a tile appears that will make him ready, even though "chow" and "pung" are usually against his principles. In this case, five tiles will serve:

1 Character: Declare "pung," meld 1-1-1 character, discard 4 character. The hand is then ready, *waiting for 3 character or 1 dot.* Or: declare "pung," meld 1-1-1 character, discard 3 character. The hand is then ready, *waiting for 2 or 5 character.*

2 Character: Declare "chow," meld 2-3-4 character, discard 3 character. The hand is then ready, *waiting for 1 character or 1 dot.*

3 Character: Declare "pung, meld 3-3-3 character, discard 4 character. The hand is then ready, *waiting for 1 character or 1 dot.*

5 Character: Declare "chow," meld 3-4-5 character, discard 3 character. The hand is then ready, *waiting for 1 character or 1 dot.*

1 Dot: Declare "pung," meld 1-1-1 dot, discard 4 character. The hand is then ready, *waiting for 1 or 3 character.* Or declare "pung," meld 1-1-1 dot, discard 3 character. The hand is then ready, *waiting for 2 or 5 character.*

A good player will recognize all these possibilities in the above hand, and will keep all the different ready structures in mind. If 1 character or 1 dot appears, giving him two alternative ways of making ready, as shown above, he will know which alternative to choose.

Recognizing All the Chances

Flexibility is all-important, especially when you are dealing with large groups of suit tiles. Learn to recognize all the different kinds of elements in the hand: divide it, mentally, in every possible way. Each arrangement will show you a different opportunity to go out. Many a player has let his chance slip, not realizing that a tile just discarded may complete his hand.

EXAMPLE 32: The hand contains two sets of three and some suit tiles:

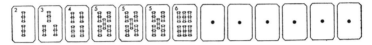

Beginner sees it this way: 2-3-4, 5-5-5, -6-. He waits for a 6.
Expert knows how to split up triplets. Also sees it this way: -2-3-4-5-6-, 5-5. He waits for a 6, or a 1 or 4 or 7.

EXAMPLE 33: The hand contains two sets of three and some suit tiles:

Beginner sees it this way: 6-6-6, -7-7-, -8-8-. He waits for a 7 or 8.
Expert also sees it this way: 6-6, 6-7-8, -7-8-. He waits for a 7 or 8, or a 6 or 9.

EXAMPLE 34: The hand contains two sets of three and some suit tiles:

Beginner sees it this way: 4-4-4, -5-, 6-6-6. He waits for a 5.
Expert mentally splits up both triplets and looks for additional possibilities: 4-4, -4-5, 6-6-6 and 4-4-4, -5-6-, 6-6. The first group needs 3 or 6; the second, 4 or 7. He waits for any tile from 3 to 7.

EXAMPLE 35: The hand contains two sets of three and some suit tiles:

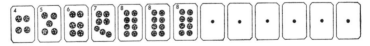

Look at it this way: -4-5-6-7-8-, 8-8. It needs 3 or 6 or 9. Now look at it this way: -4-5-6-7-, 8-8-8. It needs 4 or 7. The hand can be completed by 3, 4, 6, 7 or 9.

EXAMPLE 36: The hand contains one set of three and some suit tiles:

Look at it this way: 2-2, -2-3-4-5-6-, 7-7-7. It needs 1 or 4 or 7. Now look at it this way: 2-2-2, -3-4-5-6-7-, 7-7. It needs 2 or 5 or 8. Finally, look at it this way: 2-2-2, -3-4-5-6-, 7-7-7. It needs 3 or 6. The hand can be completed by any tile from 1 to 8.

EXAMPLE 37: The hand contains one set of three and some suit tiles:

Look at it this way: -1-1-, 1-2-3, -2-2-, 4-5-6. It needs 1 or 2. Now look at it this way: 1-1-1, 2-2, -2-3-4-5-6-. It needs 1 or 4 or 7. Finally, look at it this way: 1-1-1, 2-2-2, -3-4-5-6-. It needs 3 or 6. The hand can be completed by 1, 2, 3, 4, 6 or 7.

Ready Hands

The following are the most common ready hands. Expert players recognize them easily. III stands for a completed set of three; II stands for a completed pair; A stands for any suit or honor tile; AA or BB for any two identical suit or honor tiles, and 1, 2, 3 etc. stand for suit tiles of any one suit. The number following each example is the number of tiles theoretically available in the set that will complete the hand.

One-Chance Hands

III III III III A	needs A	3
III III III II 1-2-	needs 3	4
III III III II 2 - 4	needs 3	4

Two-Chance Hands

III III III II -2-3-	needs 1 or 4	8
III III III AA BB	needs A or B	4
III III III 1-1-1-2-	needs 2 or 3	7
III III III -8-9-9-9	needs 7 or 8	7
III III III 2 -4-4-4	needs 2 or 3	7
III III III -2-3-4-5-	needs 2 or 5	6

Three-Chance Hands

III III II -2-3-4-5-6-	needs 1 or 4 or 7	11
III III 1-2-3-4-5-6-7	needs 1 or 4 or 7	9
III III III -3-3-3-4-	needs 2 or 4 or 5	11
III III A-A-6-6-6-7-8-	needs A or 6 or 9	7

Four-Chance Hands

III III -2-3-4-5-5-5-6-	needs 1 or 4 or 6 or 7	14
III III 2-2-2-3-3-4-4-	needs 2 or 3 or 4 or 5	9
III III 4-4-4-5-5-5-6-	needs 4 or 5 or 6 or 7	9
III III 1-2-3-4-5-5-5-	needs 1 or 3 or 4 or 6	13

Five-Chance Hands

III III -2-3-4-5-6-6-6-	needs 1 or 2 or 4 or 5 or 7	17
III III -3-3-3-4-5-5-5-	needs any tile from 2 to 6	13

Six-Chance Hands

III 2-2-2-3-3-3-4-5-6-7-	needs 2 or 3 or 4 or 5 or 7 or 8	15
III -2-2-2-3-4-5-6-7-8-9	needs 1 or 3 or 4 or 6 or 7 or 9	19

Seven-Chance Hands

III 1-1-1-2-3-4-5-6-6-6-	needs any tile from 1 to 7	18
III -4-4-4-5-6-7-8-9-9-9	needs any tile from 3 to 9	18

Eight-Chance Hands

III -2-2-2-3-4-5-6-7-7-7-	needs any tile from 1 to 8	22
III -3-3-3-4-5-6-7-8-8-8-	needs any tile from 2 to 9	22

Nine-Chance Hands ("Nine Gates")

1-1-1-2-3-4-5-6-7-8-9-9-9	needs any tile from 1 to 9	23

It should be noted that the third and fourth of the two-chance hands illustrated above are virtually identical and that the same is true of the two seven-chance and the two eight-chance hands.

Improving the Ready Hand

As mentioned above, once a ready hand is made, it can, in many instances, be changed repeatedly. A one-chance hand can be changed with one draw to a two-chance hand, and with another draw to a three-chance hand, while retaining the ready state in case a tile is discarded that will enable it to go out. The examples below show how a ready hand can be changed.

EXAMPLE 38: You are the dealer in an East round. Your hand is ready. It is the tenth turn, and two East tiles have been discarded.

One chance: waiting for East. Suppose you draw 5 dot. Keep it, and discard East. It will probably not be useful to anyone else, and the evidence of the discards leads you to believe that no one else has yet made ready. Your hand is still ready, but now has two chances:

Two chances: waiting for 2 or 5 dot. Suppose you draw 6 dot. Keep it, and discard an 8 dot. The hand is still ready, but now will receive one double for no-points, and has three chances:

Three chances: waiting for 1, 4 or 7 dot. One double for no-points. Suppose you draw 6 character. Keep it, and discard 9 character. The hand now will have an additional double for all simples, and still is ready with three chances:

Three chances: waiting for 1, 4 or 7 dot. One double for no-points, and (if you go out with 4 or 7 dot) one double for all simples.

EXAMPLE 39: You are West in an East round. Your hand is ready in the ninth turn. No 2 characters have been discarded, but a four of 5's has been melded. One 3 and one 4 character have recently been discarded.

Potential score: $(20 + 8 + 4 + 0 + 0 + 0) \times 8 = 256$.

Two chances: waiting for 2 or 5 character. In reality, this is a one-chance hand: waiting for 2 character, since no 5's are available. Your chances of completing the hand are very slight, since by this time players will be avoiding "new" discards.

Suppose you draw 3 character. Keep it, and discard 4 character. The recent discard of a 4 indicates that this move is safe. Your subsequent discard may induce another player to discard a 1.

Potential score: $(20 + 8 + 4 + 0 + 0 + 2) \times 8 = 272$.

Two chances: waiting for 1 or 3 character. This is a true two-chance hand, and both 1 and 3 are likely discards.

Suppose you now draw 2 character. You can discard the 3 because the recent discard of a 3 indicates that this is safe. You have slightly reduced your chance of going out, but vastly improved the score of your hand, by adding another double for having a terminal or honor in each set.

Potential score: $(20 + 8 + 4 + 0 + 0 + 0) \times 16 = 512$. Limit: 500.
One chance: waiting for 1 character.

The above examples should make it clear that after becoming ready, one should not stop thinking. To carry the above Example 39 one step further: suppose West is your double wind. Then the second change suggested should not be made. The hand as it stands will receive the limit: at least 32 points (for the triplets) and 4 doubles (one for one suit with honors, one for the triplet of red dragons, and two for your double wind), or 512 points. Your best move is to keep the two-chance hand.

After Making Ready

A beginner will often unconsciously reveal that he has achieved a ready hand. He sighs with relief, lights a cigarette, or draws tiles in his turn without making any motion towards using them. This is an adequate signal to his opponents to size up his discards, if they have not done so before, and begin to exercise caution. To avoid other people's guessing when you are ready, do everything possible to make the other players think you are still composing your hand.

Change your hand whenever you can, even if no improvement is made, so long as you do not affect its ready state. For example if you have 6-7-8 as a complete set and you draw a 5, keep the 5-6-7 and discard the 8. Even if you know immediately that you cannot use a tile you have drawn, consider it deliberately. I am told that some Chinese players always insert a drawn tile into the hand, then remove one for discarding so cleverly that it is impossible to tell whether this is the tile drawn or not.

Declaring "Ready"

If the "ready" declaration is in use, a few things should be kept in mind. Going out after declaring "ready" gives a hand an extra double, which is of course desirable. Many players depend heavily on this technique, but it is not always advisable. Remember that, having made the declaration, you cannot change your hand; this means that you must discard every tile you draw until your hand is completed. Late in the game, this can be a perilous procedure.

When you have the option of making the declaration (that is when your hand is concealed and ready), you should consider two important questions. First, is it likely that you can go out very soon? If your hand has four completed sets and an isolated tile, the answer is no. Chances are, you will make at least five obligatory discards before getting the chance to win. Any one of these may be so advantageous to one of your opponents that it enables him to go out first. It is not wise to declare "ready" unless you have at least a two- or three-chance hand.

The second, and equally important, question is—what is the state of your opponents' hands? Is any of them ready, or is anyone making a high-scoring hand? If the answer is yes, you should probably not declare "ready." Your chances of enabling them to win, instead of yourself, are too great. If an adversary is making a one-suit hand, you should be especially cautious. Almost inevitably you will draw a tile of this suit within the next four turns. Putting yourself in the position of having to discard it may be very unwise.

Finally, your declaration naturally leaves no doubt in the minds of your opponents as to the state of your own hand. They will take stock of your discards and proceed with caution. If you anticipate that your discards will give them no revealing information, or will mislead them, "ready" may be in order. Similarly, if you have so many chances to go out that their caution will make no substantial obstacle to your winning, you may decide to go ahead. But if your discards are revealing or your opportunities to win are few, you probably should not declare.

It goes without saying that in a hand like that of East in Example 38 above, which offers many chances of improvement and gaining of additional doubles, declaring "ready" would be foolish. Only if the hand is in the best possible, or probable, condition as it stands, should the opportunity to make further changes be forfeited.

MELDING VS. WAITING TO DRAW SETS

If you meld a set at the beginning of the game, it loses all connection with your hand. If you keep it, it may form relations more useful than what you had originally planned. It is good technique, especially for the beginner, to keep all thirteen tiles concealed, unless you have very good reason to meld.

If you meld a set, your opponents immediately have a big clue as to the contents of your hand. And later, if someone else proves dangerous, you will need to have all thirteen tiles available in your hand in order to have complete flexibility in choosing safe discards.

On the other hand, it is not an absolute rule that no melds should be made, even at the beginning of the hand. One important factor in deciding is the condition of your dealt hand. If you will need only four tiles or less, the hand should probably remain concealed. If you need five, but your hand contains flexible groups of simples, there is probably no need to claim discards. Your chances of drawing the tiles you need are good. If you need five and have many isolated tiles that will have to be discarded, melding may be a good idea. Each time you claim a discard in this case, you will have a tile to discard, yourself, without loss of flexibility.

Another factor that should influence your decision is the character of the elements in your hand. A serial pair can be completed by any one of eight tiles; there should be no reason to claim a discard for it. But a pair can be completed by only two tiles. If it is important to make a triplet (as, for example, when one pair in your hand is unchangeable, since the two tiles that match it are both discarded), then "pung" should probably be declared, certainly on the second discard of the tile, if not on the first.

Finally, if the hand promises to be difficult to complete, or is a high-scoring hand, or if you have already melded and a second meld will give no additional clues to the contents of your hand, claiming discards is not necessarily wrong.

"Chow"

At the beginning of the hand, if you have no isolated tiles and many chances to draw the tiles you need, you should never declare "chow." A serial pair should almost always be completed from the wall. A separated or terminal serial pair should likewise be completed from the wall unless two or three of the tiles needed are already showing in a meld or in the discards. Only if you are making one suit only, and it is urgent that you obtain a certain tile, should you declare "chow" at the beginning. And in this case it is seldom necessary, because one-suit hands usually shape up very well through drawing.

If, on the other hand, you have isolated tiles that you can discard after melding, and your hand is otherwise good with a chance of making ready very early, "chow" may be wise.

At the end of the hand, don't declare "chow" just to make a set. It should be reserved only for the case in which you have a good chance of going out, and can make ready by melding, or for the rare occasion when someone else is collecting the suit of tiles you need and your chances of drawing them are slim. Other circumstances usually dictate that you should play for a draw.

EXAMPLE 40: In the third turn, your hand is:

Any one of the following tiles will substantially improve your hand: 5 character (discard 8); 7 character (discard 4); 5 dot (discard 9) 8 dot (discard 9); 8 bamboo (discard 9); 9 bamboo (discard 7). If any of these is discarded, don't say "chow." Count on drawing them from the wall.

EXAMPLE 41: In the third turn, your hand is:

Any of the following tiles will make you "one step before ready":
7 character
3, 4, 5 or 6 bamboo
2, 3, 4, 5, 6, 7 or 8 dot
The hand has no isolated tiles. Don't say "chow," even for 7 character, unless it has been discarded once or twice already. Count on drawing one of these from the wall. If you draw any of the bamboo or dot tiles needed, you can discard the characters.

EXAMPLE 42: In the third turn, your hand is:

This is a good hand, but 9 character and 8 dot are isolated. The plan for the hand is that the five sets will be:

2-3-4 character (need 3)
6-6 character (complete)
-2-3- bamboo (need 1 or 4)
-6-7- bamboo (need 5 or 8)
3-4-5 dot (complete)

The hand will have two doubles: no-points and all simples. It already has a pair, so it will be ready early, and probably with two chances. Declare "chow" for any of the tiles you need, especially if 3 character or 4 bamboo is discarded, and discard your own isolated tiles, 8 dot and 9 character.

"Pung"

The situation is more complicated with "pung" than with "chow." On the one hand, it should be declared more frequently in order to complete hard-to-make triplets. On the other, melds of triplets are more revealing than melds of sequences, and should therefore be avoided. Also, the question arises whether or not to claim the first discard that appears of the tile needed, or to wait for the second. Furthermore, "pung" interrupts the normal order of play, and gives the player on your right an extra turn. This should be avoided, especially if he is dealer. In addition, the discard of a tile you need indicates that, as far as the other players are concerned, that discard is safe. You have the choice between melding a triplet, or letting the discard go, and subsequently discarding your own pair.

Another factor that enters into consideration is that certain triplets bring high scores. Finally, the use of the "pung" declaration is sometimes valuable in bluffing, stalling, or otherwise opposing your adversaries. All of these factors should be weighed in each case, and the following rules should not be taken as absolute.

First Discard of Your Double Wind: Declare "pung." This gives you two doubles, and the chance should not be missed.

First Discard of a Lucky Tile: Think carefully. Almost always, depending on safety, declare "pung," because it is worth one double. But consider waiting for the second discard.

Discard of an Ordinary Wind or Terminal: Don't declare "pung" the first time. Wait for the second. If you hope to make four triplets, or if you despair of making a high-scoring hand, go ahead. But you can also let the second discard go, and then discard your own pair, or use it as the pair for the hand.

Discard of a Simple: Almost never declare "pung," even for the second discard. By melding a triplet, you make unavailable too many tiles that may be useful in other connections.

EXAMPLE 43: A 3 has been discarded. A second 3 is now discarded.

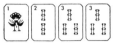

If you declare "pung," and meld your triplet of 3's, all four 3's will be unavailable. Now what will you do with the 1 and 2?

Discard by the player on your right: Think carefully. You will give him an extra turn by declaring "pung." He is your most dangerous opponent. It is better to use your pair as safe discards against him. If he is dealer, you should definitely not declare "pung," unless you have a very good reason for doing so.

Discard of your only pair: Never declare "pung." Making a triplet of the only possible pair makes a ready hand very late, and often poor. If there are no other triplets in your hand, you also lose a double for no-points by making one.

EXAMPLE 44: A 3 character is discarded.

If you say "pung," meld 3-3-3 character and discard 9 bamboo, you will have two incomplete sets left: -3-4- dot and -5-6- bamboo. Instead of waiting for one of eight tiles to complete each set, you must wait for one of eight to complete the sequence, and one of three to make the pair. Your only other choice is to discard a white dragon, and use the remaining pair. In any case, you have lost a lot of ground.

Discard after the ninth or tenth turn: It becomes increasingly unwise to declare "pung" as the hand progresses. By the tenth turn, someone is almost sure to be ready. Toward the very end of the hand, you should give up and play for a draw, using your pair as safe discards.

EXAMPLE 45: A 4 dot is discarded.

This means that 4 dot is a safe discard for you to make. It also means that 3 and 5 dot are probably very dangerous. If you declare "pung," melding the 4's, you will have to discard 3 dot, and someone will probably go out. Discard 4 dot yourself instead, because it is safe. Continue to wait for 2 or 5 dot.

Under certain special circumstances, "pung" may be wise. The following should be taken more as examples than as rules, since each individual case should be judged on its own merits.

More Than Four Pairs: If you can probably make four triplets, feel free to say "pung" early in the game, but not after the tenth turn.

Making Ready Early: If you have some isolated tiles in your hand, and an otherwise likely-looking set-up which will be ready early, feel free to say "pung," and discard an isolated tile.

Impossible Sequence: For example, if you have 3-3-4, ordinarily you should expect to make a sequence with 2 or 5. But if three or more of each are showing, feel free to say "pung" for a 3, and discard the 4. It may not be a safe discard, but you can reason as follows: the player on your right probably can not say "chow," because you have accounted for six of the neighboring tiles. If he says "pung," no one gets an extra turn. If someone else says "pung," you will get an extra turn yourself.

An Opponent Says "Chow": You can frustrate his purposes by saying "pung" and taking the tile he wanted, inasmuch as "pung" outweighs "chow."

Threes and Sevens: Sometimes it is smart to make triplets of 3's and 7's. People who have terminal serial pairs are then prevented from making sequences, at least for a long time.

Decoying: If your opponents are overly dependent on the 1-4-7 type of reasoning in defensive play (see next chapter), you can sometimes mislead them into discarding the tile you need to go out. For example, given 1-1-3-3, say "pung" for a 3, in hopes of making someone else discard a 1. Or, given 2-3-4-4, say "pung" for a 4, so that they will think 1 is a safe discard.

Stalling: At the end of the hand, "pung" is always bad unless you have reason to bluff—that is, make your opponents think you are trying to go out when in reality you have given up. In this case, say "pung" to make it appear that you are completing your hand, and lead other players to be extra cautious. But be careful yourself: you must be sure to reserve safe discards in your hand for your own use.

"Kong"

Various opportunities arise for making fours, but it is not often a good idea. The one exception is when melds have been made anyway, and an additional meld will reveal nothing, or when the substantial score of 32 for a concealed four of terminals or honors is too high to resist. In the following cases, however, "kong" probably should not be declared.

Concealed Triplet of Simples: A triplet of simples often facilitates an early ready hand. For example, 5-5-5, with a 4 or 6 makes a three-chance ready hand: 4-5-5-5 with a 3 gives 3-4-5, 5-5; with a 4 gives 4-4, 5-5-5; with a 6 gives 4-5-6, 5-5.

Several Concealed Triplets: Never make a four if you have a chance to make three or four concealed triplets.

Lucky Sets: If you have a high-scoring hand, resist the temptation to make it even higher. For example, suppose you are making a dragon hand, and have melded a triplet of red dragons. You hold a concealed triplet of white, and a pair of green dragons. If you draw a white dragon, you could make a concealed four of white, but this would warn your opponents not to discard the green dragon. Discard the white, because you know it is absolutely safe. Someone else's later discard of a green dragon will give you a limit hand.

Melded Triplet: It is usually safe to make a four, if you draw the fourth to a melded triplet early in the hand. But towards the end of the hand, resist. If someone goes out by robbing your four, you will have to pay him double his score. If you discard the tile, and he goes out, you will of course still have to pay him, but he will not have the extra double. Or if it is a suit tile, and you can keep it for use in another set, you will lose nothing.

CHAPTER THREE
Defensive Strategy

DISCARDING

Offense, not defense, is the goal of Mah Jong, and should be emphasized. In general, if you have a good hand, try to go out, being as bold as necessary about discarding as long as it is early in the game and no one is ready. If you can make ready early and well, make the best possible ready hand without worrying about defense. But if you have a late ready hand, or a hopeless one, play defensively. That is, *never give another player a tile that he needs.*

Early Discards

Your first discards will be the isolated tiles: those that have no connection with the rest of your hand. You should usually discard these in the following order:

Isolated Ordinary Winds: Wind tiles are not very valuable, except your own. A triplet gives you only 4 or 8 points. But for someone else, they are worth one double. So discard them very early, before any opponent can collect a pair of them and declare "pung" for your discard. The first discard should be the one you want least to have claimed. If you are not the dealer, discard East first. If the dealer goes out, he receives double payment anyway, and with a double for his wind he would receive four times his score. Next discard the wind of the player on your left. If he says "pung," you can draw again, and the other two players lose their turns. Then discard the winds of the players opposite you and on your right.

Beware especially of the dealer in the East round. A triplet of East will give him two doubles on top of the double for dealer. Beware also of South in the South round, West in the West round, and North in the North. The latter is almost as dangerous as East, because the North round is the last. A decisive win for him at this point could put him ahead of you for good.

In a hopeless hand, keep the wind of any skillful player, and anyone's double wind, until someone else discards it. Then follow suit immediately or not at all. A player will often collect a pair after the first discard of a tile.

Terminals: These are more useful than honors because they can combine in sequences as well as in triplets. But they are not lucky tiles. Depending on the hand, you should sometimes discard terminals, and sometimes dragons, first. The question to ask is, will you use them later or not? For example, should you discard 1 or 9 first, out of the group 1-6-9? If you get -2-3-, you can use the 1. But if you draw -7-8-, you will not need the 9, because you already have the 6. So discard the 9 first.

In deciding which suit to discard from, generally follow the rule that you should dispose of the shortest suit first. For example, if you have 1-5 bamboo and 1-5-6-8-9 character, discard 1 bamboo. Your hand may shape up for one suit with honors.

Dragons: These are not as valuable as the beginner may think. For one thing, they are hard to collect. For another, if kept too long, they become dangerous to discard. It is usually best to discard them early, in order to prevent your opponents from making sets of them. In any case, *decide immediately* what you will do. It may be disappointing to draw a second one immediately after you have discarded the first, but it happens to the best of players.

Of course you should always keep pairs of dragons. But isolated ones should be discarded immediately or not at all. In a good hand, discard one or two immediately after the dangerous winds. If you have three, wait to discard one of them after one or two terminals, in order that it may not be obvious to your opponents that you have a good hand. In a hopeless hand, keep them all from the beginning, to prevent absolutely anyone else's making a triplet.

Special Winds: Of the two special winds, the prevailing wind is usually more difficult to collect than your own, since it brings a bonus to anyone. Like the dragons, these should be discarded early or never. One good policy is to discard the prevailing wind early, but keep your own wind until it has been discarded at least twice by other players. If by then you still don't have a pair, you can discard it with reasonable safety. But beware after the ninth or tenth turn because someone may make ready using it for a pair.

Your double wind is extremely valuable to you. A triplet is worth as much as a whole hand conforming to one suit with honors, or no-points with all simples. Except in very rare cases, keep it for a long time, until you see it has been discarded twice or even three times and will be utterly useless to you or anyone else.

Simples: These are very useful, and can form connections in many ways. 5 is the best of all, 4 and 6 next, 3 and 7 next, and so on. So keep 4, 5 and

6 as long as you can. They should be the last isolated tiles to discard in almost every hand. *But*, if you have five good elements already, and can not anticipate using the isolated simples, discard them early. Or if you have an excellent chance of making all terminal or honor sets, discard them early. In fact, if you are sure you will not use them, they should be the first to go.

Later Discards

Until about the tenth turn, the best policy is to discard dangerous tiles early. At about the tenth round, someone is likely to have become ready, and your tactics should change accordingly. Many tiles that were safe at the beginning are now dangerous. Winds are dangerous, because by now your opponents may have pairs of them. Terminals and dragons are dangerous because by now someone may be waiting to complete his pair and go out. Simples are especially dangerous, since every hand by now has elements for sets they want to complete.

By this time also, your own hand has probably shaped up reasonably well, and you must choose which of several related tiles to discard. You should decide on two bases: first—"What is most useful for me to keep?" and second—"What is the least dangerous to discard?" At this point, the second question should begin to take precedence over the first.

The best way to decide whether a specific tile is dangerous or not is to examine the discards of your opponents, as explained more fully below. Here, however, are a few general rules that are useful but not always completely dependable:

Given 2-4-4, discard the 2. Your chances of drawing another 4 are half as good as your chances of drawing a 3, but you can use the pair of 4's as they are, and 2 is usually a safer discard than 4.

Given 1-2-4, discard the 1, which is safer than 4, because you must wait for a 3 in any case.

Given several serial pairs and a triplet, discard one member of the triplet. It is probably safe, because no one else can be holding a pair of these tiles, and you can use the remaining pair as it is.

Given many good elements, discard pairs rather than serial elements. Pairs are safer to discard, and more difficult to form into triplets. If you discard a pair of 2's, the danger is only that someone else may be holding a similar pair, which is unlikely. If you discard a 2 and 3, you are in double danger. Someone may be holding a pair of 2's *or* a pair of 3's.

At about the sixth or seventh round of play, you should begin to examine carefully the discards of your opponents, and ascertain what kind of tiles they are collecting. By the ninth or tenth discard, you should know pretty well what is in every other player's hand. You should also be able to tell when a player becomes ready, and exercise great caution from then on, especially if you yourself are not ready.

WATCHING THE TABLE

The Player on the Right

Your most dangerous opponent is the player on your right. He is the only one who can use your discards to complete his sequences, by saying "chow." You will find that it is he, most often, who uses a suit tile you discarded. Whenever this happens, he is closer, by one set, to going out, and you are more likely to have to pay him for winning. Remember that it is ultimately just as bad to allow a player to complete a set as it is to give him the chance to go out. Each complete set puts him one step further ahead of you. So, especially when discarding suit tiles, play defensively against the player on your right.

Watch his discards. *Early in the game,* the suit tiles he discards are probably isolated ones; their near neighbors are safe. Later, the suit tiles probably come from elements; their near neighbors are dangerous. Thus, in Example 46 below, you can assume that he has no bamboo tiles, and probably no low characters. The 7 character discard was late, and may have come from a 6-7-7 or 7-7-8 combination, in which case the tiles 5 through 9 are dangerous. All dot tiles are dangerous. The later bamboo discards were probably drawn late. In Example 47, high dots and probably low ones are safe. In Example 48, low characters are obviously safe; high ones are dangerous; dot tiles, certainly toward the ends, are safe.

Still considering the player on your right *at mid-game,* his elements will probably be serial pairs, and usually he will not have separated pairs, pairs, or single tiles in a ready hand. Assuming this, you can use the following as general rules to aid you in picking your discards:

If he discards	You can discard
1	1
9	9
2	2 (and probably 1)
8	8 (and probably 9)
3	3 (and probably 1 and 2)
7	7 (and probably 8 and 9)
4	1 and 4 (and probably 2 and 3)
6	6 and 9 (and probably 7 and 8)
5	2 and 5 and 8

Each of these rules can be reasoned logically. To explain one of them as an example: suppose the player on your right has discarded a 6. *Assuming that he has serial pairs only*, and does not have a pair, separated pair or isolated tile in his hand, you can be sure that the serial pair concerned is not -4-5-

or -7-8-. If it were, he would have kept the 6 to make a sequence. These are the serial pairs that he could have: 1-2-, -2-3-, -3-4-, (not -4-5-), -5-6-, -6-7-, (not -7-8-), -8-9. These serial pairs can be completed respectively by 3, 1 or 4, 2 or 5, 4 or 7, 5 or 8, 7. Therefore he does not need a 6 or a 9.

These rules are useful, but do not overtrust them. If you have no absolutely safe discard, use them. But if your opponent is a clever player, it may well be that it is exactly these tiles which are most dangerous. He can trap you, for example, by discarding a 5, and making ready with a separated serial pair, 7-9, in hopes that you will discard an 8.

This logic can be applied as well to the other players' discards, and you should begin to be careful of them at about the tenth round of play. But you should play defensively against the player on your right from the very beginning.

Counting Tiles

Another, and often more reliable way to determine safe discards is to count the number of tiles showing. With honors, which can only be combined into triplets or pairs, the reasoning is simple: if three of them are showing on the board, either discarded or melded, the fourth is a safe discard. With suit tiles, you must count the tile in question and its adjacent tiles on both sides, in order to be sure you can discard one safely. For example, 1 is a safe discard if three 1's and four 3's are showing, or of course if three 1's and four 2's are showing. A 5 is safe if three 5's, four 4's and four 7's are showing (or four 3's and 6's, or four 4's and 6's). Since you can seldom have such absolute assurance, you must often reason as in the following examples:

Four 3 characters have been discarded. No one can make a 1-2-3 sequence. 1 and 2 are safe unless someone has a pair of 1's or 2's to make a triplet, or is ready and waiting with an isolated 1 or 2.

Four 3 characters, two 2's and two 1's are discarded. You are holding a 1 and a 2. Therefore, no one can make a 1-2-3 sequence, nor can anyone be holding a pair of 1's or 2's. 1 and 2 are safe unless someone is ready and waiting with an isolated 1 or 2.

Opponents' Discards

Finally, you can learn a lot in general from the trend of your opponents' discards. Here again, experience is the best teacher. An American who played Mah Jong in China tells the following story:

"Somehow the adversary on his left will persistently discard tiles which are of no earthly use to him, while the adversary on his right will repeatedly bury in the discard the very tiles he wishes to chow but can't. Even if he has a run of good luck in the draw and gets his hand down to two pairs he may sit waiting for either a four or six of bamboos, let us say, to match either of his pairs, when presently his left-hand adversary will lay down a completed hand—all in characters except for a four-five-six bamboo sequence, which contains both the tiles that the American is calling. Hard luck, doubtless. What our American fails to understand is that his seemingly scattered and meaningless discards have been a succession of revelations of what tiles he doesn't want until his watchful adversaries, by an intricate series of deductions, know perfectly well what he does want, and refuse to discard it. The amazing skill that some Chinese have developed in this business of inference and deduction, until after eight or nine rounds of the draw they can read with amazing accuracy the make-up of all three opposing hands, is the whole art of Mah Jong." (Hartman, Lee Foster: *Standardized Mah Jong*)

Piecing together an opponent's hand from his discards is an interesting pursuit. When learning the technique, it is a good idea to make a guess at each other player's hand; then at the end of each hand, examine it to see how close your guess was. This way you will learn what pitfalls to avoid when depending on deduction. Here are a few hints:

Absence of One Suit: If his discards are predominantly of two suits, beware of the third. With the player on your right, you can find out if the third suit is dangerous by investigating early in the game. Discard a tile of that suit which you don't need. If he declares "chow," never discard that suit again.

Early and Late Suit Discards: Early: when he discards a suit tile, its near neighbors are probably safe. His discard was probably an isolated tile. Late: when he discards a suit tile, its near neighbors are probably dangerous. His discard was probably part of an uncompleted element.

Threes and Sevens: "Threes and sevens are hard to get." Don't discard them until the player on your right does. The reason is that they are the only suit tiles which can be used for both terminal sequences and for simple sequences. Thus they are often needed both by people who are collecting terminals, and by people who are eliminating terminals from their hands.

High, Low, and Middle Numbers: In any one suit, if his early discards are high numbers, he probably has a group of low numbers, and vice versa. If his discards are middle numbers, apply the suggested rules, but watch out for the end tiles not covered by them. For example, if he discards a 5, 8 may be safe, but 7 and 9 are not.

Double Wind: If he discards his double wind early in the game, he probably hopes to make a very high hand.

Complete Sequence: If he discards a whole sequence in three or four consecutive turns, he is probably making a one-suit hand.

Danger Signs

Under certain circumstances, a good Mah Jong player will be particularly cautious. This is when an opponent has made two or three melds which give evidence of an extremely high-scoring or limit hand:

Three Melds of One Suit: Under no circumstances should you discard any tile of that suit.

One Meld of Lucky Tiles and Two of One Suit: Under no circumstances should you discard any honor, or any tile of that suit.

Two Melds of Dragons: Under no circumstances should you discard the third dragon.

Three Melds of Winds: Under no circumstances should you discard the fourth wind.

Three Melds of Honors: Under no circumstances should you discard any honor.

Three Melds of Terminals: Under no circumstances should you discard any terminal if the three melded terminals are triplets. Terminal sequences also indicate a hand with at least one double, but this is not a limit hand and is not so dangerous to abet.

Three Melds of Green Tiles: If "all green" is counted as a limit hand, under no circumstances should you discard any green tile.

In fact, in the above cases it is wisest to limit your discards, whenever possible, to tiles that are identical to those your opponent has discarded.

How to Detect a Ready Hand

In general, you can discern what kind of hand a person is making from his early discards. Then, when the first discard which looks like part of his hand appears, it often means that he is ready.

EXAMPLE 46: In his eleventh turn, your opponent's discards are these:

His first ten discards are honors, bamboos and characters. His eleventh is a dot tile. You can conclude that he is collecting dot tiles predominantly, and probably high characters, and that he is probably ready.

EXAMPLE 47: In his ninth turn, your opponent's discards are these:

His first eight discards are honors and dot tiles. His ninth is a low character. You can conclude that he is collecting bamboos, and probably character tiles, and that he is ready.

EXAMPLE 48: In his ninth turn, your opponent's discards are these:

His first seven discards are terminals and low character tiles. His eighth is a high character, which you saw him take out of his hand while he kept what he drew. Surely he would not have harbored this terminal for so long unless it was part of a group? He may be ready—or nearly ready. His ninth discard is a bamboo that also came out of his hand. He must be ready, and is probably waiting for 6 or 9 bamboo.

EXAMPLE 49: The story of a mistake, taken from an actual game.

Player North, a beginner at Mah Jong, starts with six character tiles in his hand, and his two draws are additional characters. He has a complete 2-3-4 dot sequence, and no honors except for isolated West and North tiles. He decides to make a one-suit-only hand, and after discarding his isolated tiles, starts to discard the sequence in his fourth turn. In his seventh turn, South becomes ready. In his eighth turn, he makes a four of 9 characters and discards a 4 bamboo, enabling East to make a 4 bamboo triplet and make ready. In his ninth turn, West becomes ready.

North still has three tiles to go. In fact he needs to make a complete character set. He keeps drawing additional dot tiles, preserving his character sequence in spite of himself, and doggedly continues discarding dot tiles. In his twelfth turn, he discards the 2 dot tile that enables West to go out.

At this time, North's hand was as follows:

Obviously, even from the point of view of his own hand, 2 dot was an un-wise discard. His previous discards were:

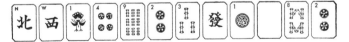

He should have known better. The evidence of his opponents' discards indicates that any of them might be able to use 2 dot. It also suggests that they are all ready, and that he should give up. He should have begun to play defensively in his tenth turn, and begun to use his 3 characters as safe discards, following South discard of 3 character. His hand, in fact, was filled with safe discards, and he could easily have avoided losing, if he had realized it.

East's discards:

East's melds:

Obviously, East is not collecting character tiles, judging from his first suit-discard. The 6 character was an isolated tile; it was the logical discard after the honors. The two dot discards indicate that he is not collecting high (though he may want low) dot tiles. His "pung" for 4 bamboo and subsequent discard of 1 bamboo indicate that he made ready with this move. Subsequent discards, which North should have noted, all came from the wall. The import:

Avoid low dots and all bamboos

South's discards:

South's meld:

Obviously, South is not collecting characters, since he has discarded 2, 3, 4, 5, 6 and 8 characters. His early high bamboo discards suggest that low bamboos may be dangerous. He has discarded no dots. When he claimed 2 dot from East and melded 1-2-3 dot, he discarded his own wind. This was a good indication that he had made ready and saw no reason to hold it any longer. The import:

Avoid low bamboos and all dots

West's discards:

West's melds: none.

West may be collecting characters, but he has not claimed any from the variety in South's discards. As far as West is concerned, character discards are probably safe. His bamboo discards are 6 - 9 - 3 - 5, in that order, and probably indicate that he is not collecting bamboo. But after a final honor discard, he kept a drawn tile and discarded 3 dot. The import:

Avoid all dots, especially low ones

These are the actual hands, at which North could have guessed with fair accuracy:
East's hand:

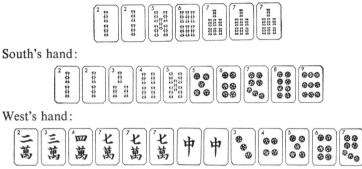

South's hand:

West's hand:

East is waiting for 2, 4 or 7 bamboo; South is waiting for 4 or 7 dot; West for 2, 5 or 8 dot. Thus, of the dot suit, 2, 4, 5, 7 and 8 should have been avoided. North, who was holding 2, 3 and 7 at this time, decided simply to discard them in that order. The 3 was safe, but had he discarded the 7, East would have gone out.

OPPOSING A SINGLE PLAYER

The Player on the Left

He treats you as you treat the player on your right. The best policy is to try to deceive him by use of the 1-4-7 principle. For example, if you have 1-3-5, discard the 5 if you can do so safely, and trick him into discarding 2. Or if you have 5-6-8-9, discard 9 and 8 in hopes that he will discard a 7. If he is making a big hand, overcall his "chow" with "pung" whenever you can.

The Player Opposite

He is difficult to get at. The best you can do is to overcall his "chow" with "pung" whenever you can. Or if you see that he is discarding one kind of tile predominantly, for example, characters, try to make ready waiting for a tile of that suit.

If either of the above two players seems to be making a big hand, and your own is hopeless, it is sometimes wise to help the player on your right by discarding tiles that he can use. Better for him to go out cheaply than for someone else to score the limit. But this is rarely advisable.

The Dealer

The three non-dealers should cooperate against him, because he gets double score. North is the most responsible, however, because it is his discards that the dealer can claim for sequences. When you are North, never claim a tile except for a lucky triplet, because you will give him an extra turn. Go out cheaply. When you are attempting a big hand, your discards are apt to be too indiscriminate.

DEDUCTION AND PSYCHOLOGY

The above description of deductive methods may seem to leave a lot to chance. In Example 49 above, we concluded that the discard of a character tile would not have been dangerous—when West actually had six character tiles in his hand. The reader's inference could be that our deductions were not sound.

True, the absence or presence of certain tiles in a player's discards, and this alone, is not sufficient ground on which to found an absolutely secure conclusion as to the contents of his hand. But there is an additional aid at the disposal of any player who wishes to use it, which often makes sure an otherwise uncertain guess: the expressions on the faces of his adversaries.

It is almost impossible to keep from betraying an interest in certain tiles as they are discarded, and the clues offered by this interest are innumerable. If North had watched, he would have seen that each of the character tiles discarded by South brought only an indifferent glance from West, while at his own dot discards, both South and West looked with interest. The observation would confirm the assumption that any character discard would be safe with respect to his opponents.

The number of conclusions that can be drawn from observations of this kind is astounding. Consider the behavior of a player in his turn. If he draws, glances at, and discards a tile, you can be sure he holds no tiles connected with it. If he does this with 8 dot, for example, you know immediately that a 7 or 9 dot discard is safe, and that probably a 6 is too.

If he draws, hesitates, and discards a tile, he may have a group related to it, but the group is probably complete. Then, with 8 dot, the group is probably a 7-8-9 sequence, a triplet or pair of 7's or 9's, or possibly a 6-7-8 sequence or triplet of 6's. At any rate, high dot discards, from 7 up are safe as far as he is concerned. If you yourself are waiting for a 7, and three are already showing on the board, this is the time to change your plans. The fourth 7 is almost undoubtedly in his hand.

If he draws, and keeps the tile, then discards unhesitatingly another from his hand, you know he is probably not yet ready. But if he draws, deliberates, and discards a tile which has no relation to the trend of his previous discards, he is ready, probably waiting for a near relation of the tile just discarded. From now on, that suit or the kind of tiles in which he shows especial interest should be scrupulously avoided by you.

It follows that, with observant opponents, it is precisely the opposite kind of behavior that you should cultivate. Show interest in bamboos when you are waiting for characters; discard hesitantly the tiles that do not have any connection with your hand, and negligently those that do. When playing for a draw, seek to make it appear, if possible, that you are making a high hand. Discard a whole sequence of one suit (which your right-hand adversary, as you judge from his discards, will not be able to use) in three consecutive turns, and avoid altogether the discards of one suit—the one you least wish to see discarded by any other player. The techniques are endless.

Consider another type of reasoning similar to that discussed above. An example will best serve to illustrate it. The player on your right is making a big hand. He has melded a set of dragons, a triplet of his own wind, and a triplet of 6 bamboos. He has discarded miscellaneous honors, terminals, and character and dot tiles. Upon melding the triplet of 6 bamboos, he discards a 7 bamboo, with no hesitation, which means he must be ready.

You yourself are one step before ready, and now draw the tile that completes your ready hand. But you want to discard an 8 bamboo. Is it safe? Counting the melds and discards, you see that three 3's, two 4's, three 5's, one 7, two 8's and one 9 are unaccounted-for. You know from his previous move that he must have discarded the 7 from a 6-6-7 combination, and that of the four tiles remaining in his hand, two must be paired and two can be in sequence or paired. If both had been in sequence, he would not have made a triplet of his only possible pair—the 6's. The only possible pairs are 3's, 4's, 5's and 8's. But you are holding an 8. Therefore, if he is holding two pairs, he has 3's, 4's or 5's.

If he is holding a pair and a sequence element, what elements could he complete with your 8 discard? The only possible sequence elements that could be completed by an 8 are -6-7- and 7--9. It can't be -6-7-, because he has melded three 6's and the fourth is discarded. But it could be 7--9. Thus far, pure reasoning would take you. If he had a pair and 7-7--9, however, *he would have hesitated* before discarding, trying to decide whether to hold two pairs (4-4, say, and 7-7) or a pair and sequence-element (4-4 and 7--9). He discarded without hesitating—and so you conclude that he is holding two pairs, of the three possibilities, 3, 4 or 5, and that your 7 discard is safe. You discard 7 bamboo, and subsequently go out. When he reveals his hand, your opponent displays two pairs: 3-3 and 5-5.

It remains to be said that I have not covered even half of the techniques used by skillful Japanese players of the game. The more skillful you and your opponents become, the more varied are the possibilities for psychological strategy, deception, adroit manipulation of the tiles, and endless other techniques. The fascinations offered by Mah Jong increase with every round of play, and the very fact that they cannot be summarized on paper proves that it is a game to play and not to analyze.

Diagram of a Complete Game (see page 33)

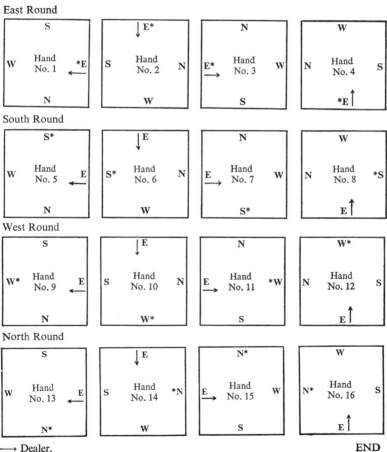

East Round

South Round

West Round

North Round

——→ Dealer.

   * This player has the double wind.

END

Glossary-Index

Glossary-Index

This glossary-index, in addition to explaining all of the terms used in this manual, includes those that are used exclusively in the American Code, in which case they are indicated with the initials "AC."

All rules quoted herein are those of the Japan Mah Jong Association.

Also included for those who are interested, but by no means as a prerequisite for the full enjoyment of the game, are the Chinese expressions commonly used in the Orient, including Japan. In those instances where the Japanese use a particular expression of their own, this is clearly indicated.

The pronunciation of the Chinese expressions are transliterations based on Japanese usage and therefore players familiar with the Chinese language may find them slightly inaccurate in some instances. In any case, the differences between direct Chinese-to-English transliteration and mine are consistent throughout, and once familiar with these differences the reader should be able to convert my terms easily to the proper Chinese pronunciation.

Since Chinese "r" and "1" sounds are usually transliterated as "1," and Japanese "r" and "1" sounds as "r," I have had to choose one or the other in each case. I have translated both "r" and "1" as "r" throughout, with the single exception of "lon," which the Japanese pronounce clearly with an "1" sound. The same problem arises with "f" and "h." This sound, when followed by "an," or "u," will be found under "f." When followed by "a" or "o" it has been rendered as an "h."

Accessories, 18, 64

Adaptability, 101

All green *(ryuu ii sō)*. A limit hand according to the *American Code*. 89, 92

All honors *(tsuu ii sō)*. A winning hand containing only honor tiles. It scores the limit. 40, 57, 88, 92, 93, 94

Cleared hand in the AC, 94

Doubles, 93, 94

All kongs (AC). *See* "Four fours."

All-sequence hand (AC). *See* "No-points."

All simples *(tan yao chuu;* sometimes called *tan yō* by the Japanese). A winning hand containing only suit tiles from number two to eight, including no terminals or honors. It is given one double. 39, 53, 85, 115

All terminals *(chin rao tō)*. A winning hand containing only terminal tiles and no simples or honors. It scores the limit. 40, 57, 92, 93, 94

Cleared hand in the AC, 94

All terminals and honors *(hon rao tō)*. A winning hand containing both terminal and honor tiles, but no simples. It receives one double in addition to whatever doubles may be acquired from the individual sets. This is a cleared hand according to the AC. 39, 54, 91, 93, 94, 95, 118

American scoring rules, 90-95

An kan 暗槓 Concealed four.

An kō 暗刻 Concealed triplet.

Arrangement of hand, 67, 105

Average hand, 114

Bakkin (Japanese) 罰金 Penalties.

Bamboos *(sō tsu)*. The thirty-six suit tiles bearing pictures of bamboo sticks, sometimes with a bird or a bamboo shoot for number one, numbered one to nine. 17

Big four winds *(taa suu shii)*. A winning hand, containing one triplet of each of the four winds. It scores the limit. The AC term is "Four large blessings." 40, 57, 85

Big three dragons *(taa san yuan;* often called *dai san gen* by the Japanese). A winning hand containing one triplet of each of the three dragons. It scores the limit. The AC term is "Three great scholars." 40, 57, 85, 92

Blessings (AC). *See* "Little four winds," and "Big four winds."

Bones *(chō ma;* sometimes called *ten bo* by the Japanese). A set of ivory or plastic sticks used as counting accessories to the Mah Jong set. They are given point values and used like poker chips for scoring. *See also* "Initial points." 18, 37

Bonus for dealer's extra hand. A popular Japanese addition to the game, not officially sanctioned. 70

Bouquet (AC). When the flower and/or season tiles are used, a combination of them that gives four doubles to a hand. 79, 91

Breaking the wall. The procedure by which it is determined where in the wall the deal should begin. The dice are thrown by the dealer; the indicated player throws again, and the two numbers thrown are added. The sum of the two numbers indicates the number of stacks that should be counted off from the right end of the latter player's row before making the break. 24, 65

Building the wall *(chii pai)*. The procedure by which the tiles are stacked into rows before each hand of play. Each player builds a row of seventeen stacks, and pushes the row toward the center to meet, at the corners, the other players' rows. 23, 63

Call (AC). The American equivalent of the "ready" declaration. *See* "Delayed Call."

Calling (AC). *See* "Ready," and "Waiting."

Calling hand (AC). *See* "Ready hand."

"Chan-chan." The Japanese expression for the drawing of two tiles, by the dealer, after he has drawn a hand of twelve tiles. The two are taken from the top of the wall, skipping one.

Chan kan 槍槓 Robbing a kong.

Chan tai yao 全帶公 Terminal or honor in each set.

Chances

  Making ready, 126

  Recognizing of, 124

Characters *(wan tsu)*. The thirty-six suit tiles bearing Chinese characters for the numbers one to nine. 17

Chen 千 One thousand. The Japanese variant is *sen.*

"Chii" 吃 "Chow."

Chii cha 起家 First dealer.

Chii hō 地和 Earthly hand.

Chii pai 砌牌 Building the wall.

Chii toi tsu 七対子 Seven pairs.

Chin chowan 井圈 Wall.

Chin ii sō 清一色 (清一) One suit only. The Japanese variants are *chin itsu* and *chin ichi.*

Chin rao tō 清老頭 All terminals.

Chō ma 籌和 Bones. The Japanese variant is *ten bō.*

Chon hō 冲和 Mistake in going out.

Chow. Claiming a discard that completes a sequence. After chowing the player must meld his completed sequence. A player may chow only in his own turn, claiming the discard of the player on his left.

  Strategy, 130

"Chow" *("Chii")*. The declaration made when claiming a discard in order to complete a sequence. 28

Chowan cha 莊家 Dealer. The Japanese variant is *sō cha.*

Chowan hon 莊風 Prevailing wind.

Chowan tsu 莊子 Discs.

Chun 中 Red dragon. *See also "Hon chun."*

Chun chan pai 中張碑 Simples.

Chun ren pao ton 九連宝灯 Nine gates.

Circles. *See* "Dots."

Cleared hand (AC). *See* "One suit only," "One suit with honors," "All terminals and honors," "All honors," and "All terminals."

Cleared-hand game (AC). An American variant of Mah Jong in which the above-mentioned hands are the only ones allowed. 11, 94, 95

Dragons *(san yuan pai; yuan pai)*. The twelve honor tiles called "red dragons," "white dragons" and "green dragons." There are four of each. A set of any of them earns a winner one double. 18, 41
Draw (of a tile) *(tsuu mō; mō pai)*. The first move in a player's turn, consisting of taking a tile from the wall for possible use in his hand. Drawing can be foregone in order to claim a discard to chow, pung or kong.
Draw (ending hand of play) *(pin chui)*. A hand won by no one. Five kinds of draws used to be recognized in Japan, known by the following names: *suu kai kan* (four fours), *suu hon tsu ren ta* (four same discards), *tao pai* (nine different honors and terminals in the dealt hand), *howan pai* (no one goes out), and *san cha hō* (three people declare "out"). 32
Drawn hand. *See* "Dealt hand."
Earthly hand *(chii hō)*. A winning hand belonging to a non-dealer, who goes out either on the dealer's first discard or on a self-drawn tile in his first turn. It scores the limit. 40, 58, 92
East player *(ton cha)*. The dealer, whose position is always East.
East round *(ton hon)*. The first round of the game, consisting of four (not counting extra) hands of play. During this round, East is the prevailing wind. 148

Four (cont.)

Lucky fours, 39, 45, 91

Making fours, 30

Four concealed triplets *(suu an kō)*. A winning hand containing four triplets, all of whose tiles were drawn from the wall. It scores the limit. The AC term for this is "hidden treasure." 39, 40, 47, 57, 80, 92, 117

Four flowers, 79, 91

Four large blessings (AC). *See* "Big four winds."

Four small blessings (AC). *See* "Little four winds."

Four triplets *(toi toi hō)*. A winning hand containing four triplets, which is variously scored. It receives one double, or, if three triplets are concealed, two doubles. If all four are concealed, it is a limit hand. 39, 47, 80, 91, 117

Four-winds hand *(suu shii hō)*. The Japanese make no distinction in scoring between "Big four winds" and "Little four winds," so both hands are given the same name.

Big four winds, 40, 57, 85

Little four winds, 40, 57, 85, 91, 92

Freedom of count. The rule that a player who has two alternative ways of scoring the last tile of his hand may pick the way that gives him the higher score. It is assumed to be understood in this book. 42

Fu ri ten 振り聴 Sacred discard.

Fuu 副 Points.

Fuu rō 副露 Melding.

Fuu rō pai 副露牌— Melds and discards.

Fuu tei 副底 The 20 points for winning.

Game *(ii chowan)*. A complete game of Mah Jong consisting of four rounds or sixteen hands of play, not counting the dealer's extra hands. The AC term is "round of the winds." 33, 148

Gates, Nine, 40, 58, 92, 119

Goal, 27

Going out *(hō ra)*. Completing the hand and declaring "out." This constitutes winning. The AC term is "Mah-Jong." "Woo" is also used by some authorities. 31

By robbing a kong *(chan kan)*. A winning hand that goes out by taking a tile just added to a melded triplet by another player who wishes to make a four. It receives one double. The AC makes this a limit hand if the tile taken happens to be 2 bamboo. This is called *ryan sō chan kan*. 31, 39, 49, 91

Rules, 31

Self-drawn *(tsuu mō hō)*, 39, 41, 59

With discard *(lon hō)*, 39, 41, 59

Going out (cont.)

With last tile of wall *(hai tei rao yue;* in Japanese dialect, *hai tei rō ei).* A winning hand that goes out with the last tile before the dead wall. It receives one double. The AC makes this a limit hand if the tile taken happens to be 1 dot. This is called *ii ton rao yue.* 39, 48, 91

With last discarded tile *(hō tei rao yui).* A winning hand that goes out on a tile discarded after the last tile of the wall has been drawn. It receives one double. The AC makes this a limit hand if the tile taken happens to be 1 dot. This is called *ii ton rao yui.* 39, 49, 91

With supplement tile *(rin shan kai hō).* A winning hand that goes out on a supplement tile from the dead wall, after making a four. It receives one double. The AC makes this a limit hand if the tile taken happens to be 5 dot. This is called *uu ton kai hō.* 39, 49, 91

Green dragon *(hatsŭ sai; ryuu ha;* often called *hatsu* by the Japanese). The four honor tiles with a green Chinese character on them. 18, 41

Green tiles, 142

Ground (AC). *See* "Meld."

Grounded set (AC). *See* "Melded four," "Melded sequence," "Melded triplet."

Hai tei pai 海底牌 Last tile of wall.

Hai tei rao yue 海底捞月 Going out with last tile of wall. Japanese variant: *hai tei rō ei.*

Hai tei rō ei (Japanese) 海底捞月 Going out with last tile of wall.

Haku (Japanese) 白 White dragon. *See also "Pai pan."*

Hand (a player's) *(pin pai; shō pai).* The thirteen tiles held by a player during the game. When he goes out it is called a winning hand.

All green, 89, 92

All honors, 40, 57, 88, 92, 93, 94

All kongs, 92

All simples, 39, 53, 85, 115

All terminals, 40, 57, 92

All terminals and honors, 39, 54, 91, 93, 94, 95, 118

Arrangement, 67, 105

Average, 114

Big four winds, 40, 57, 92

Big three dragons, 40, 57, 85

Concealed, 39, 42, 46-47, 79-81

Dealer's extra, 32, 70, 89

Dealt, 26, 63, 109

Displaying, 32, 36, 68

Eighth extra, 89

Hand from heaven (AC). *See* "Heavenly hand."

Hatsu 発 Green dragon. *See also "Hatsu sai."*

Hatsu sai 発財 Green dragon.

Heavenly hand *(ten hō)*. A winning hand held by the dealer that goes out as dealt before a discard has been made. This scores the limit. The AC term is "Hand from heaven." 40, 58, 92

Heavenly twins. A limit hand, as defined in the AC. 87, 92

Hidden treasure (AC). *See* "Four concealed triplets."

History of the game, 9

Hō chon 和種 Hand name.

Hō pai 和牌 Last tile of hand.

Hō pai 花牌 Flowers and seasons

Hō ra 和了 Going out.

Hō tei rao yui 河底撈魚 Going out with last discarded tile.

Hon 風 Wind. The Chinese use this word to mean a "round" of play.

Hon chun 紅中 Red dragon, often called *chun* by the Japanese.

Hon ii sō 混一色 One suit with honors. Japanese variants: *hon itsu; hon ichi.*

Hon pai 風碑 Wind tiles. *See also "Suu hon pai."*

Hon rao tō 混老頭 All terminals and honors.

Honor or terminal in each set, 39, 54, 85, 118

Honors *(tsuu pai.* The honors and terminals are collectively called *yao chuu pai)*. The twenty-eight honor tilesc alled dragons and winds. 18, 39

    All honors,   40, 57, 88, 92, 93, 94

Honors and terminals, Five pairs, 39, 118

Hopeless hand, 112

Howan pai 荒牌 No one goes out. The officially recognized condition for declaring a draw.

Ii cha pao 一家色 Discarder pays. The rule that the player who discards the winning tile must pay for all three losers.

Ii chii ton kan 一気通貫 Three consecutive sequences. Japanese variant: *ikkitsuu kan.*

Ii chowan 一荘 Game.

Ii chuu pai 一九牌 Terminals. *See also "Rao tō pai."*

Ii fan shiba-ri (Japanese) 一飜縛り One-double game.

Ii shan ten 一向聴 One before ready.

Ii shun 一順 Sequence held in the hand during play.

Ii ton rao yue (yui) 一筒撈魚 Going out with last tile of wall or last discarded tile when that tile is 1 dot.

Ikkitsuu kan (Japanese) 一気通貫 Three consecutive sequences. *See "Ii chii ton kan."*

Impossible sequence, 134

Initial points. The value of the bones dealt to each player before the start of the play, officially set at 2000. 38, 78

Insurance penalties. Rules applying to the situation when a player makes a limit hand possible for another player during the game, now seldom used. 75

Ippei kō (Japanese) 通二順 Two identical sequences. *See "Ton ryan shun."*

Isolated tile. Any tile held in the hand that has no relation to the other tiles of the hand. This is considered an element. 105

Jan tō 雀頭 The pair that makes up the fifth set of a completed hand.

Japan Mah Jong Association, 10

Jongg. The round box in which the discs, *q.v.*, are found in the Mah Jong set. It is sometimes used instead of the dice to indicate who is dealing, and is passed when the deal passes. 64

Judging dealt hand, 109

"Kan" 槓 *"Kong."*

Kan chan machi 嵌張待 Waiting for middle of sequence.

Kan taa 嵌塔 Separated serial pair.

Kan tsu 槓子 Four.

Kaze pai (Japanese) 風牌 *See "Suu hon pai."*

Kō shii uu showan 国士無雙 Thirteen orphans. Japanese variant: *koku shi mu sō.*

Kō tsu 刻子 Triplet.

Koku shi mu sō (Japanese) 国士無雙 Thirteen orphans.

Kong. Making a four, either by adding a discard to a concealed triplet or by adding a drawn tile, to either a concealed or a melded triplet.
  Melding, 30
  Robbing, 31, 39, 49, 91
  Strategy, 134-135

"Kong" *("Kan")*. The declaration made when making a four.

Kong on kong. A limit hand according to the AC. 88, 92

Last discarded tile. A tile discarded after the last tile of the wall has been drawn. 39, 48, 91

Last tile of hand *(hō pai)*. The fourteenth tile acquired by a winning hand. It is worth 2 points if it was drawn from the wall, and 2 points if it completed a one-chance hand. 39, 41, 79

Last tile of wall *(hai tei pai)*. The last playable tile of the wall, excluding the fourteen tiles that compose the dead wall. If a player goes out with this tile, he receives one double. 39, 48, 91

Limit *(man gan)*. The maximum score, officially set at 500 points per hand. Certain special hands automatically score the limit. 38, 78

Limit hand. A winning hand that automatically, or by virtue of its high score, receives the limit. 40, 56-59, 87-89, 92

Limit hand (cont.)

Little four winds *(shao suu shii)*. A winning hand, containing one triplet of each of three winds and a pair of the fourth. It scores the limit. The AC term is "four small blessings." 40, 57, 85, 91, 92

Little three dragons *(shao san yuan;* often called *shō san gen* by the Japanese). A winning hand containing one triplet of each of two dragons, and a pair of the third. It receives one double in addition to those acquired from the dragon triplets. The AC term is "three small scholars." 39, 56, 84, 85, 91

"Lon" 粜 "Out."

Lon chowan 輪荘 Passing the deal.

Lon hō 粜和 Going out with a discarded tile.

Long hand *(taa pai)*. A hand that has more than thirteen tiles (plus one for each four), by mistake. Such a hand may not go out. It is sometimes called a dead hand. 33

Looking ahead, 109

Loose tiles. It used to be the custom to establish two loose tiles on top of the dead wall, for use as supplements. *See* "Supplement tiles." 66

Losers, Settlement among, 90, 93, 94

Low hand, 114

Luck, 101-104

Lucky set *(fan pai)*. A triplet or four composed of lucky tiles. Each lucky set in a winning hand earns the hand one double. 39, 135

    Doubles, 39, 45-46, 79-80, 91, 93, 94

    Fours, 39, 45, 91

    Triplets, 39, 45, 91

Lucky tiles *(fan pai)*. The three dragon tiles, the prevailing wind and, for each player, his own wind. 40, 41

Mah-Jong (AC). *See* "Going out."

Make ready. To bring a hand within one tile of going out. To make a ready hand. *See also* "Ready." 121-128

    Early, 121, 134

Man (Japanese) 万 Ten thousand. *See also "Wan."*

Man gan 満貫 Limit; limit hand.

Matching tile with serial pairs, 106

Meld *(fuu rō* is a verb. The noun, which includes both melds and discards, is *fuu rō pai* or *rō pai.)* The act of exposing face-up on the table a set that was completed by claiming a discard. Also the set so treated. The AC term is "ground."

    Advisability, 130

    "Chow," 28, 130

    Danger signs, 142

    "Kong," 30

    "Pung," 29

    Vs. drawing, 130

Melded four *(min kan)*. A four, one of whose tiles was a discard claimed by punging or konging. It is displayed on the table with all four tiles face up. The AC term is "grounded four." 30, 39, 40, 67

Melded sequence *(shun tsu)*. A sequence one of whose tiles was a discard claimed by chowing. It is displayed face up on the table. The AC term is "grounded sequence." 28, 67, 83

Melded triplet *(min kō)*. A triplet one of whose tiles was a discard claimed by punging. It is displayed face up on the table. The AC term is "grounded triplet." 29, 39, 40, 67, 135

Men hon 門風 Own wind.

Men tsu 面子 Element.

Men zen chin 門前清 Concealed hand.

Men zen tsuu mō 門前自模 Concealed self-drawn hand.

Min kan 明槓 Melded four.

Min kō 明刻 Melded triplet.

Mistake. The four different kinds of mistakes, in play, are given special names: *tsuo chii* (mistake in chowing); *tsuo pon* (mistake in punging); *tsuo kan* (mistake in konging); and *tsuo hō* or *chon hō* (mistake in going out). 33

Mixed-hand game, American, 10, 91

Mō pai 模碑 Draw (a tile).

Moon from the bottom of the sea. A literal translation of the Oriental term for going out with the last tile of the wall. 88, 92

Nan cha 南家 South player.

Nan hon 南風 South round.

Nine gates *(chuu ren pao ton)*. A concealed winning hand, all of one suit, containing a triplet of ones, a triplet of nines, a run from two to eight, and whose last tile matches any of these. It scores the limit. 40, 58, 92, 119

No-points *(pin fuu)*. A winning hand that has no points. It contains four sequences and a pair of non-lucky tiles. It went out with a discarded tile, and was not a one-chance hand. It receives one double. The AC term is "all-sequence hand." 39, 50-53, 84, 91, 116

Non-dealers *(san cha)*. The three players whose positions are South, West and North. Their hands are scored differently from the dealer's, hence the distinction. 22

North player *(pei cha)*. The player whose position is to the left of the dealer. His wind is North.

North round *(pei hon)*. The fourth round of the game, consisting of four (not counting extra) hands of play. During this round North is the prevailing wind. 148

Offensive strategy, 105-135

One before ready *(ii shan ten)*. The name given by Oriental players to a hand that lacks one tile of being ready to go out, that is, it lacks two tiles of being a winning hand. 123

One-chance hand. A winning hand that goes out either by obtaining: a) the second tile of its pair; b) the middle tile of a sequence; or c) the inside tile of a terminal sequence (the 3 of 1-2-3 or the 7 of 7-8-9). Completing a one-chance hand is worth two points. These three hands are given individual names by the Chinese and Japanese. The AC term is "filling only place." *See also* "Waiting." 39, 41, 42

One-double game *(ii fan shiba-ri)*. A variant of Mah Jong in which every winning hand must have at least one double. This AC variant is popular in Japan. 11, 93

Pung. Claiming a discard that completes a triplet. After punging, the player must meld his completed triplet. 28, 67

Strategy, 132-134

"Pung" ("Pon"). The declaration made when claiming a discard in order to complete a triplet. 28

Rao tō pai 老頭牌 Terminals. Japanese variant: ii chuu pai.

Ready (ten pai). When a player's hand requires only one tile to go out, it is said to be ready. The AC term is "calling." 31

Declaration ("Rii chi"). An optional addition to the game, popular in Japan, and official in one form in America. The AC term is "call" or "delayed call." 71, 129

Doubles, 71, 85, 91

Hand (ten pai). A hand that requires only one tile to go out. 31, 71, 126-128

Detection of, 142

Improvement of, 127-128

Making ready, Early, 121, 134

Payment, 89

Techniques, 122

Red dragon (hon chun; chun). The four honor tiles with a red Chinese character on them. 18, 41

Redeal. If the players agree that the dealer may deal again after a draw, the hand is called a redeal, in contradistinction to a dealer's extra hand. 70

Ren chowan; ren chan 連莊 Dealer's extra hand.

Ren hon 連風 Double wind.

"Rii chi" 立直 "Ready" declaration.

Riichi Mah Jong, 12, 70

Rin shan kai hō 嶺上開花 Going out with a supplement tile.

Rō pai 露牌 Melds and discards. See also "Fuu rō pai."

Robbing a kong (chan kan). If a player draws a tile and adds it to a melded triplet to make a melded four, and if another player can go out on this tile, he may do so. This is called "robbing a kong," and receives one double. The AC makes this a limit hand if the tile taken happens to be a 2 bamboo, in which case it is called ryan sō chan kan. 31, 39, 49, 91

Round (hon). A round consists of four hands of play, not counting the dealer's extra hands. It ends when each of the four players has once held and lost the deal. The Chinese word hon means "wind." 33

Round of the winds (AC). See "Game."

Rounding-off the score, 37, 60, 90

Ryan men machi 両面待 Waiting for a two-ended sequence.

Ryan sō chan kan 二索槍槓 Going out by robbing a kong when the tile taken is 2 bamboo.

Ryuu ha 緑発 Green dragon. *See also "Hatsu sai,"* and *"Hatsu."*

Ryuu ii sō. 緑一色 All green.

Sacred discard *(fu ri ten)*. A tile among a player's discards that is identical to one that he needs in order to go out. He may not claim a tile identical to it until he has drawn at least once from the wall subsequent to his own discard. 31, 72-74

"Sacred discard" declaration *("Fu ri ten")*. An optional rule permits a player to go out on a discarded tile identical to one of his own discards, if he has previously declared "sacred discard." 73

Sai zu (Japanese) 骰子 Dice. *See also "Shai tsu."*

Sample game, 101

San an kō 三暗刻 Three concealed triplets.

San cha 散家 Non-dealers.

San cha hō 三家花 The situation whereby three people declare "out." One of the conditions for declaring a draw according to the old rules.

San kan tsu 三槓子 Three fours.

San shoku dō jun (Japanese) 三色同順 Three similar sequences, sometimes just called *san shoku*. *See also "San sō ton shun."*

San shoku dō kō (Japanese) 三色同刻 Three similar triplets, sometimes just called *san shoku*. *See also "San sō ton kō."*

San sō ton kō 三色同刻 Three similar triplets. Japanese variants: *san shoku dō ko* and *san shoku*.

San sō ton shun 三色同順 Three similar sequences. Japanese variants: *san shoku dō jun* and *san shoku*.

San yuan pai 三元牌 Dragons, sometimes simply called *yuan pai*.

Scholars (AC). *See* "Little three dragons," and "Big three dragons."

Score

    Final, 37

    Rounding off, 37, 59, 90

    Total, 37

Scoring

    American rules, 90-95

    Outline, 38

    Procedure, 36-60, 78-89

    Table, 39, 91

        American mixed-hand game, 91

Scratching a carrying pole *(ryan sō chan kan)*. A limit hand as defined by the AC. 88, 92

Seasons. Tiles previously used in Mah Jong, no longer officially recognized.

    Bouquets, 79

    Doubles, 79-80

    Points, 79

Shan pon machi 雙碰待 Waiting for triplet.

Shao pai 少牌 Short hand.

Shao san yuan 小三元 Little three dragons. Japanese variant: *shō san gen.*

Shao suu shii 小四喜 Little four winds. Also called *suu shii hō.*

Shii cha 西家 West player. Japanese variant: *sha cha.*

Shii hon 西風 West round. Japanese variant: *sha hon.*

Shii pai 洗牌 Shuffle.

Shii san yao chuu 十三么九 Thirteen orphans. More commonly used, however, is *kō shii uu showan.* Japanese variant: *koku shi mu sō.*

Sho pai 手牌 A player's hand. Also called *pin pai.*

Sho san gen (Japanese) 小三元 Little three dragons. *See also "Shao san yuan."*

Short hand *(shao pai).* A hand that has less than thirteen tiles (plus one for each four) in it, by mistake. Such a hand may not go out. Sometimes called a "dead hand." 33

Shuffle *(shii pai).* The procedure by which the tiles are mixed before building the wall. The term is not used in this book.

Shun tsu 順子 A sequence, melded or concealed, that is displayed in a winning hand.

Shuu pai 数牌 Suit tiles.

Simples (chun chan pai). The suit tiles, excepting the ones and nines, i.e. all tiles numbered two, three, and so on up through eight.   39, 40, 53, 85, 115

    Concealed triplet,   39, 40, 134

    Defensive strategy,   137

Skill,   101-104

Sō cha (Japanese) 莊家 Dealer. *See also "Chowan cha."*

Sō tsu 索子 Bamboos.

South player *(nan cha).* The player whose position is to the right of the dealer. His wind is South.

South round *(nan hon).* The second round of the game, consisting of four (not counting extra) hands of play. During this round South is the prevailing wind.   148

Special inclusions,   39, 50, 81

Special winds,   137

Stack. A pile of two tiles, forming a unit in the wall.   24

Stalling,   111, 134

Strategy   95-148

    Defensive,   136-148

    Offensive,   105-135

Suits *(shuu pai).* The hundred and eight tiles called "bamboos," "characters" and "dots."   17

Supplement tiles. The tiles composing the dead wall, which may be drawn only to supplement a player's hand after he has made a four. The term "loose tiles," used in the AC, has roughly the same meaning. 30, 39, 49, 65, 91

Suu an kō 四暗刻 Four concealed triplets.

Suu hon pai 四風牌 Wind tiles. Sometimes simply referred to as *hon pai*. Japanese variant: *kaze pai*.

Suu hon tsu ren ta 四風子連打 Four same discards, one of the situations in which a draw was declared according to the old rules.

Suu kai kan 四開槓 Four fours made by more than one player, one of the situations in which a draw was declared according to the old rules.

Suu kan tsu 四槓子 Four fours made by one player.

Suu shii hō 四喜和 Four-winds hand. See also *"Taa suu shii,"* and *"Shao suu shii."*

Taa pai 多牌 Long hand.

Taa pai 打牌 Discarding.

Taa san yuan 大三元 Big three dragons. Japanese variant: *dai san gen.*

Taa suu shii 大四喜 Big four winds, also called *suu shii hō.*

Taa tsu 塔子 Serial pair.

Tan chao machi 単吊待 Waiting for a pair.

Tan yao chuu 断么九 All simples. Japanese variant: *tan yō.*

Tan yō (Japanese) 断么 All simples. *See also "Tan yao chuu."*

Tao pai 倒牌 Nine of the *yao chuu pai* (terminals and honor tiles) in a dealt hand. One of the situations in which a draw was declared according to the old rules.

Temporary East. The seat temporarily named East by the first throw of the dice in the game. After the players draw for seats, the one who draws East sits in the temporary East seat. Two subsequent throws of the dice select the game's first dealer, and the "temporary East" designation is then permanently dropped. 21

Ten bō (Japanese) 点棒 Bones. *See also "Chō ma."*

Ten hō 天和 Heavenly hand.

Ten pai 聴牌 Ready; ready hand.

Ten thousand. *(wan—*Chinese; *man—*Japanese). The character that appears on each of the character tiles, the meaning of which is "ten thousand."

Terminal or honor in each set *(chan tai yao).* A winning hand containing simples, but which has at least one terminal in every set of suit tiles. It scores one double. 39, 54, 85, 118

Terminal serial pair, 106

Terminals *(rao tō pai;* sometimes called *ii chuu pai* by the Japanese). All the suit tiles numbered one or nine. The terminals and honors together are called *yao chuu pai.* 18, 39

Ton hon 東風 East round.

Ton ryan shun 通二順 Two identical sequences. *Ippei-kō* in Japanese.

Ton san shun 通三順 Three identical sequences.

Ton tsu 筒子 Dots. See also *"Pin tsu."*

Tournament play, 33, 34

Triplet *(kō tsu).* A set of three identical tiles, sometimes called "three-of-a-kind." 27

Triplets

    Double wind, 39, 45, 91

    Four, 39, 47, 80, 91

      Concealed,   40, 47, 57, 80, 91, 92, 117

    Lucky,   39, 45, 91

    Making,   28

    Melded,   29, 39, 40, 67, 135

    Several concealed,   39, 47, 48, 80, 91, 135

    Simples, concealed,   39, 40, 134

    Three concealed,   48, 80

    Three similer,   82

Tsuo chii 錯吃 Mistake in chowing.

Tsuo hō 錯和 Mistake in going out. *See also "Chon hō."*

Tsuo kan 錯槓 Mistake in konging.

Tsuo pon 錯碰 Mistake in punging.

Tsuu ii sō 字一色 All honors.

Tsuu mō 自模 Drawing from the wall.

Tsuu mō hachi pin fuu 自模八平和 Self-drawn eighty.

Tsuu mō hō 自模和 Self-drawn.

Tsuu pai 字牌 Honors.

Two identical sequences *(ton ryan shun;* called *ippei kō* by the Japanese). 83

Uu ton kai hō 五筒開花 Going out with a supplement tile when that tile is 5 dot.

Waiting. The following are the Oriental terms for the various kinds of ready hands. The AC term is "calling."

    For end of sequence (a ready hand whose incomplete set is a terminal serial pair): *pen chan machi.* 42, 126

    For middle of sequence (a ready hand whose incomplete set is a separated serial pair): *kan chan machi.* 41, 126

    For a pair (a ready hand whose incomplete set is an isolated tile): *tan chao machi.* 41, 126

    For a triplet (a ready hand whose incomplete set is a pair): *shan pon machi.* 126

Waiting (cont.)

For two-ended sequence (a ready hand whose incomplete set is a serial pair): *ryan men machi.* 126

Wall *(chin chowan).* The arrangement of the tiles, during play, in rows around the table, stacked two-high. Sometimes called "pile."

Breaking, 24, 65

Building, 23, 63

Dead, 26

Wan 万 Ten thousand. Japanese variant: *man.*

Wan pai 王牌 Dead wall.

Wan tsu 万子 Characters.

Washing, the tiles (AC). The procedure by which the tiles are mixed before building the wall.

Ways of going out, Doubles for, 39, 48-50, 81, 91

West player *(shii cha;* called *sha cha* in Japanese). The player whose position is opposite the dealer. His wind is West.

West round *(shii hon;* called *sha hon* in Japanese). The third round of the game, consisting of four (not counting extra) hands of play. During this round West is the prevailing wind. 148

White dragon *(pai pan;* called *haku* by most Japanese). The four honor tiles with blank white faces. 18, 41

Wind

Double, 33, 39, 41, 45, 91, 141

Own, 33, 41

Prevailing, 33, 41

Winds *(suu hon pai; hon pai;* sometimes *kaze pai* in Japanese). The sixteen honor tiles called East, South, West and North. 18

Big four, 40, 57, 85

Little four, 40, 57, 85, 91

Ordinary, Isolated, 136

Special, Defensive strategy, 137

Winner, Paying the, 37, 59, 69, 89-90, 93, 94

Winning hand. A completed hand that has gone out.

Winning points, 38-40, 91

Winning tile. The last tile of a winning hand, obtained by claiming the discard of another player. The discarder of the winning tile must pay the whole loss to the winner. 37, 39

Woo (AC). *See* "Going out"

Yao aru 幺二 Terminal and honor tiles.

Yao chuu pai 幺九牌 Terminal and honor tiles.

Yuan pai 元牌 Dragon tiles. See also *"San yuan pai."*

SCORING TABLE

POINTS

Winning 20

Sets

Sequences 0
Melded triplets
  Simples 2
  Terminals or honors 4
Concealed triplets
  Simples 4
  Terminals or honors 8
Melded fours
  Simples 8
  Terminals or honors 16
Concealed fours
  Simples 16
  Terminals or honors 32
Pairs
  Suit tiles 0
  Ordinary winds 0
  Lucky tiles 2
  Double wind 4

Last Tile of Hand

Discarded 0
Self-drawn 2
One-chance 2

Concealed Hand

With discarded tile 10
With self-drawn tile (see *Doubles,*
at right.)

DOUBLES

Lucky Sets
Loucky triplet or four 1
Double wind triplet or four .. 2

Concealed Hand
With discarded tile (10 points)
With self-drawn tile 1

Groups of Sets
Four triplets, including fours
  0, 1 or 2 concealed 1
  3 concealed 2
  4 concealed .... limit
Three concealed triplets with
  one sequence 1

Ways of Going Out
Last tile of wall 1
Last discarded tile 1
Robbing a kong 1
Supplement tile 1

Special inclusions
Three consecutive sequences .. 1

No-points 1

Consistency
All simples 1
All terminals and honors 1
Terminal or honor in each set.. 1
One suit with honors 1
One suit only 4
Little three dragons 1

LIMIT HANDS

Big three dragons
Little four winds
Big four winds
All honors
All terminals

Four concealed triplets
Heavenly hand
Earthly hand
Nine gates
Thirteen orphans